AUTOMOBILES
THAT CHANGED HISTORY

METRO BOOKS
New York

Contents

Introduction

Automotive technology continues to evolve by leaps and bounds. Today we can enjoy and benefit from innovations that only a few decades ago would have seemed like the fantasies of a mad scientist. But progress also means immense energy and financial investment to enhance research and promote development. This is why, in an increasingly aggressive and ruthless global market, car manufacturers are frantically seeking value for their money, the convergence of ideas, standardization, economies of scale and alliances. This financially responsible approach, however, inevitably leads to products that are blander and very similar.

Evening out the competitive landscape also helps standardize the inescapable laws of aerodynamics and ergonomics, plus the equally unavoidable regulations regarding emissions and safety, which demand convenient and cheap techniques that produce consistent results.

Thirty, forty, fifty years ago, these constraints did not exist. Industrial and economic logic was less pressing, leaving a lot of room for genius, imagination and taste.

The differences between one model and another, even among those belonging to the same class, could be seemingly infinite. This led to extraordinarily charismatic cars that jumped out from the crowd and created unique styles, imposed revolutionary concepts and ultimately earned a chapter in the history of the car and in the memories of fans.

Cars like the Fiat 500, the Alfa Romeo Duetto, the Volkswagen Beetle, the Mini and the Citroën 2CV are now legends and have become both a part of the culture of their time and icons for the brands they represent. Their myths – of reliability, elegance, sportiness, safety – have been used by carmakers to build up an image which, in many cases, was carried over to subsequent models.

But myths, as marketing strategists have long understood, must be maintained and cultivated through repetition – either ongoing or episodic, in winks, evocations and suggestions – provided this is in harmony with the changing needs of an automotive industry that now allows little freedom to maneuver.

Unlike the past, the technical differences between cars today are often blurred, making a strong link with a former glory a truly distinctive element, like an extra gear that drives sales and, at times, creates fads.

Cultivating this tradition can mean perpetuating a name and a philosophical point of view, as is the case for the Golf. Or it can mean simply maintaining and updating a style that's true to its beginnings, like Jeep, Land Rover and Porsche. There are also the loud and flashy comebacks which characterized the last decade. The New Beetle started this trend, followed closely by the BMW MINI and the new Fiat 500.

Cars that have stood the test of time with their original spirit intact are few and far between. To complete this book we have considered those that are the richest in meaning, with one goal – we wanted to tell good stories. Put simply, the stories that follow deserve to be known, both by the people who buy or have bought these cars and those who simply admire them.

After all, next to all the technology in your garage, there should be some space left for even a touch of meaning and history.

---

1 The Beetle is probably the most easily recognizable car of all time. For this reason, Volkswagen saw fit to replicate it in 1998.

2-3 Aston Martin is one of the car manufacturers most tied to a constant stylistic concept. The shape of the grill on the Vanquish, produced from 2001 to 2007, and other modern models, for example, has only slightly evolved from the era of the 1950 DB2.

4-5 The first Ferrari California was one of the most desirable roadsters in the world, a status symbol that collectors go crazy for even today.

6-7 The size of the 1957 500 was much smaller and the mechanical base completely different, but today's version owes its success to the fact that it has faithfully recreated the original's design.

9 A view of early models of Rolls-Royce cars in 1957. A radiator shaped like a Greek temple; a statue depicting the "Spirit of Ecstasy," inspired from the "Victory of Samothrace:" Rolls Royce has built an image around these since the beginning of the 20th century.

10-11 The Porsche 356 was born in 1948, its style conditioned and influenced by the experiments undertaken with the Volkswagen

Beetle. The Porsche style has since made its own name and is still recognizable in today's 911.

12-13 The fame of the 1962 American Chevrolet Corvette reached Europe thanks to the consistency of the mechanics and a manufacturing philosophy that has never betrayed its roots.

14-15 Ever since 1957, when Ferrari released its gem, California is a name that has captured the imagination of generations of sports car fans. Now it is also the name of the "small" 2008 offering from Maranello.

Rolls-Royce Phantom

Silence is golden

"Strive for perfection in everything you do. Take the best that exists and make it better. When it does not exist, design it." Rolls-Royce's initial goal was ambitious but also centered on the ideas of the brilliant engineer Henry Royce and financed in the first decades of the 20th century by a wealthy car-obsessed nobleman, Charles Rolls.

Since its beginning in 1906, the English carmaker has always built some of the most exclusive cars in the world. Comfort, luxury and performance are all at the highest levels without being excessive. Preserving tradition is also important. Current models, for example, are called "Ghost" and "Phantom," names used before the Second World War to highlight the "silent" qualities of British cars.

The first Phantom replaced the Silver Ghost in 1925 and had a home-made chassis, which was the Rolls custom up to the '60s, while the body was built to the specific needs of wealthy clientel by outside companies. Produced in the U.K. and the U.S. with a 7700 cc, 6-cylinder engine, you can see one of these Phantoms in the movie *The Great Gastby* (1974).

The second series in 1929 was at the root of a cinematic automotive mistake. In the film *Indiana Jones and the Last Crusade* (1989), the sultan of Hatay details the technical characteristics of the car but completely mistakes the engine's displacement, which is the same as the previous generation, but is described as a "4300."

18-19 The "Spirit of Ecstasy" statuette has adorned the hoods of Rolls-Royce cars since 1911. Up until 1914 it was plated in silver, which was eventually replaced by a nickel alloy meant to discourage theft.

The most famous example of the Phantom on the big screen is probably the yellow and black version from the third series produced from 1936 to 1939 owned by James Bond's legendary enemy, Auric Goldfinger, the villain of the 1964 film named after him.

Once production resumed following World War II, Rolls-Royce brought its most exclusive car ever to market in 1950 – the Phantom IV. Only 18 Phantom IVs, with a 5700 cc, 8-cylinder engine, were made, all of which were destined to end up in the hands of

royalty and heads of state like the Shah of Persia and the Aga Khan. Even today, models belonging to England's Queen Elizabeth and Spain's King Juan Carlos are used in official ceremonies.

This exclusive customer base continued with the fifth generation from 1959 to 1968. The 516 units produced were mainly purchased by monarchs, including Queen Elizabeth, the Queen Mother and King Olaf of Norway. The decidedly non-royal John Lennon ordered a white one, which he dutifully decorated with psychedelic colors.

The British monarchy's fleet of cars still includes two six series (1968–1991) Phantoms. The "Silver Jubilee Car," created in 1978 to celebrate the 25th anniversary of the coronation of Elizabeth II, features a reproduction of St. George killing the dragon in place of the "Spirit of Ecstasy," which is the traditional Rolls-Royce hood ornament.

One of the 374 produced, which came with dual zone climate control for independent temperature management between the front and rear seats, is now the official car of the governor of Australia.

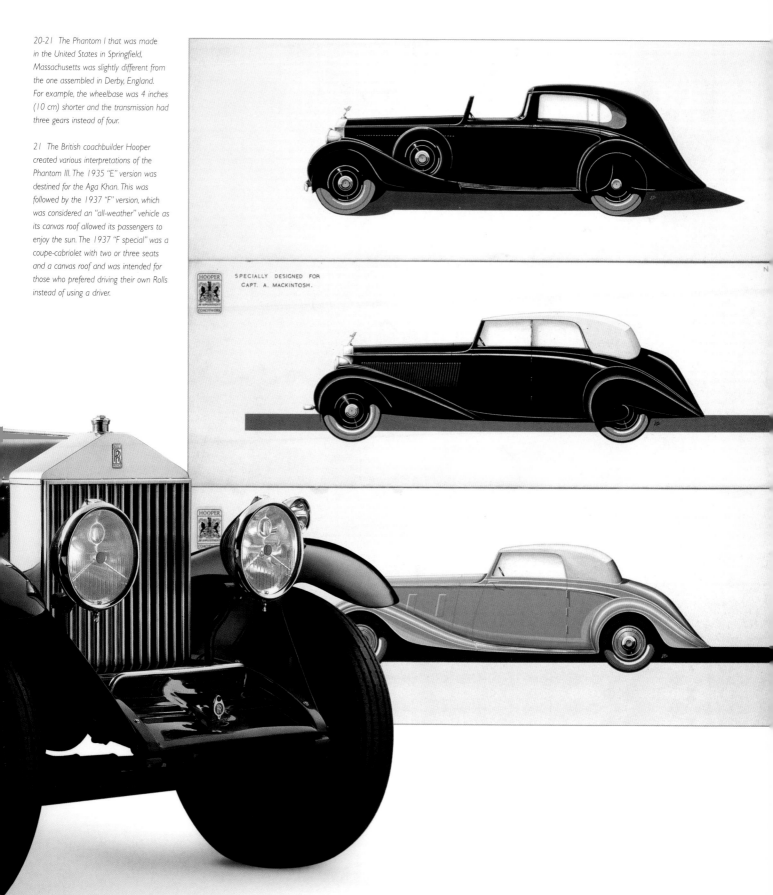

20-21 The Phantom I that was made in the United States in Springfield, Massachusetts was slightly different from the one assembled in Derby, England. For example, the wheelbase was 4 inches (10 cm) shorter and the transmission had three gears instead of four.

21 The British coachbuilder Hooper created various interpretations of the Phantom III. The 1935 "E" version was destined for the Aga Khan. This was followed by the 1937 "F" version, which was considered an "all-weather" vehicle as its canvas roof allowed its passengers to enjoy the sun. The 1937 "F special" was a coupe-cabriolet with two or three seats and a canvas roof and was intended for those who prefered driving their own Rolls instead of using a driver.

SPECIALLY DESIGNED FOR
CAPT. A. MACKINTOSH.

22-23 The 1964 movie The Yellow Rolls-Royce told the story of three Phantom II owners: an English aristocrat (Rex Harrison), a Chicago gangster (George C. Scott) and an American widow (Ingrid Bergman). Seen here is Shirley MacLaine, another star of the film, getting out of the car.

23 Two stars of the 1974 film The Great Gatsby: a 1928 Rolls-Royce Phantom I and Robert Redford. The movie won Oscars for costume design and best original score. The car was sold to an unnamed collector at a 2009 auction for $238,000.

24-25 *One of the most fascinating versions of the Phantom II, built between 1929 and 1936 in both convertible and hard top, is the Continental, which was sportier than its sisters thanks to an engine with a high compression ratio. In all, 281 Continentals were produced.*

25 *The convertible version of the Continental is a rare sight, as only two were ever produced. The one pictured is from 1931 and has belonged to a private collection since 1989. The other car, with coachwork by Thrupp and Maberly, is from 1934 and was owned, along with other great cars, by the American actor Tyrone Power.*

Dimensions fit for a king

The spectacular Phantom of our day, propelled by a 12-cylinder, 460 hp engine, was born in 2003 with the help of BMW, which has owned the British brand since 1998. Despite less-than-noble origins – 15% of its components, including the engine, comes from BMW's flagship 7 Series – the Rolls-Royce philosophy has not been disrupted. Assembly is still done by hand and the two robots staffing the Good-wood factory have only one task – paint the body.

Among the car's idiosyncrasies is the absence of a tachometer (replaced by a power reserve dial, which indicates how much power is still available), rear-hinged back doors which allow enough space to accommodate an umbrella, a retractable hood orna-ment that prevents theft and protects pedestrians in the event of an accident and a Rolls-Royce logo in the heart of the alloy wheels that remains fixed, even when the car is moving and the wheels are turning.

The arrival of the 2007 convertible version called the Drophead and the 2008 coupe helped modernize the list of customers that traditionally purchase the Phantom. Celebrities like David Beck-ham, Denzel Washington and Nicolas Cage, who has nine, are all new Phantom owners.

As Lord Rolls said, "After the price is forgotten, quality endures." In the case of the Phantom, as in all Rolls-Royces, he who asks how much it costs can't afford it.

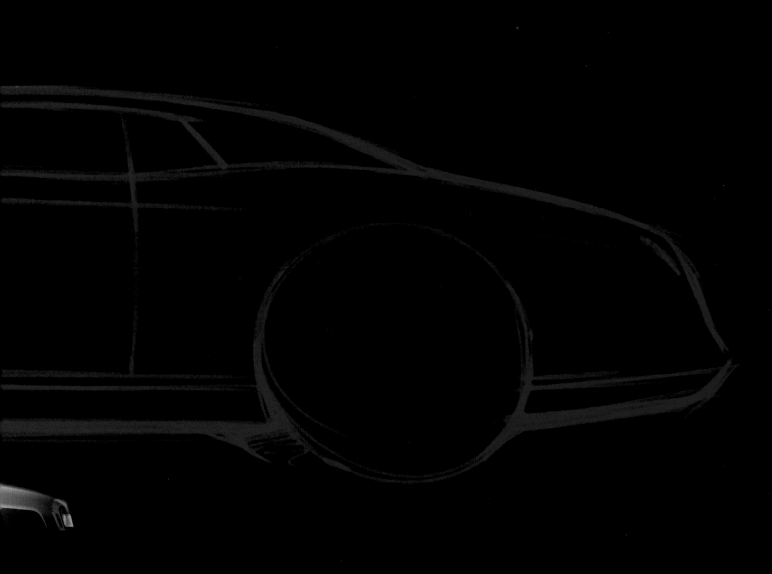

26-27 The 2008 Phantom Coupe is the most recent Rolls-Royce and the third model since BMW bought the carmaker in 1998. The designers wanted to give the car a touch more sportiness without losing the traditional elegance of the Phantom sedan.

26 bottom The arrival of the coupe and convertible versions of the Phantom helped rejuvenate the image of Rolls-Royce, which has always attracted a more mature audience. Today, the English cars are increasingly in demand by singers, actors and athletes.

28-29 top from left One of the most prominent stylistic and functional elements of the *Phantom Drophead Coupe* was the windshield frame, which incorporated uprights. Very thick and in brushed metal, it provided a great sense of security. This stage of the design process shows the asymmetrical front end, which let designers compare and contrast various technological options. For headlights, the Phantom designers chose to adopt the solution seen at the right. With such a monumentally large body, it wasn't easy for designers to manage a streamlined style, so the work of "streamlining" was conducted on the side contours of the car.

28 bottom and 28-29 bottom The Phantom convertible was also held in high regard for the comfort it provided the rear passengers. Space in the rear passenger compartment was excellent. Doors closed automatically and the lining of the roof could even be outfitted with small LED lights that resembled stars. The coupe uses the same 12-cylinder 460 hp BMW engine equipped in the sedan and convertible combined with a 6-speed automatic transmission. With its improved aerodynamics, the Phantom can now hit a top speed of 155 mph (250 km/h).

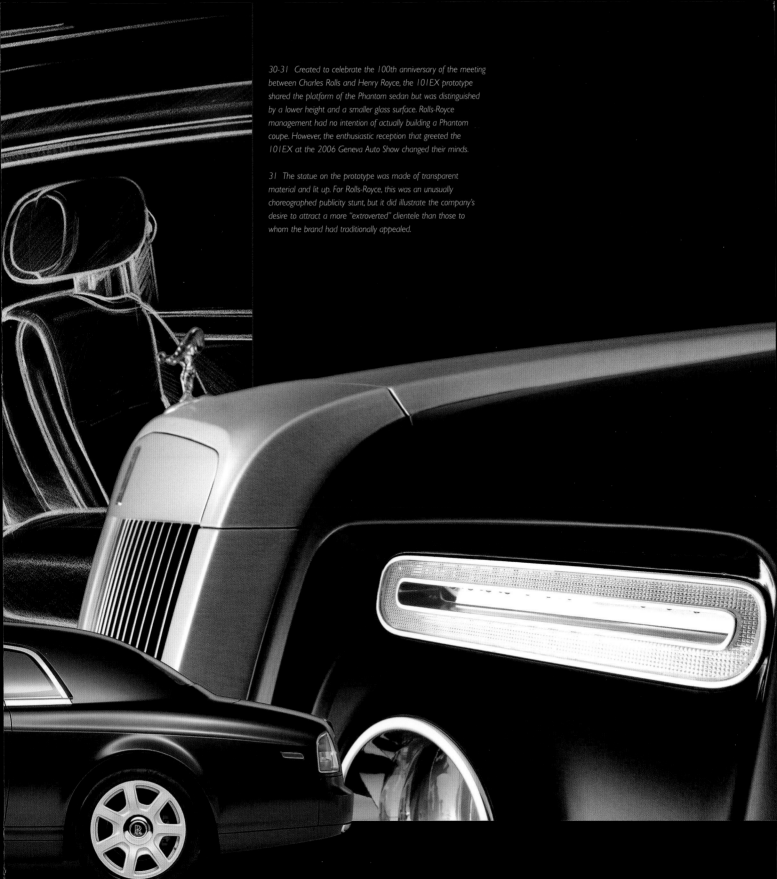

30-31 Created to celebrate the 100th anniversary of the meeting between Charles Rolls and Henry Royce, the 101EX prototype shared the platform of the Phantom sedan but was distinguished by a lower height and a smaller glass surface. Rolls-Royce management had no intention of actually building a Phantom coupe. However, the enthusiastic reception that greeted the 101EX at the 2006 Geneva Auto Show changed their minds.

31 The statue on the prototype was made of transparent material and lit up. For Rolls-Royce, this was an unusually choreographed publicity stunt, but it did illustrate the company's desire to attract a more "extroverted" clientele than those to whom the brand had traditionally appealed.

Alfa Romeo 8C

The "sublime" car

In 2003, Alfa Romeo needed to restore its sophisticated image after years of products that had progressively moved it away from its own tradition and closer to the general standards of Fiat, which has owned the Lombardy-based brand since 1986. Thus, at the Frankfurt Auto Show, Alfa Romeo presented a nostalgiac prototype that recalled the style of its racing cars of the '60s, such as the 33 Coupe Stradale and the Giulia TZ, and that had an equally evocative name: the 8C Competizione.

8C, short for "8-cylinder engine," was reminiscent of a series of extraordinary cars in the 1930s that brought the Alfa brand to world attention. The first of these was the 8C 2300 that was the result of designer Vittorio Jano's experiences with the 1924 P2 racer, which had an 8-cylinder engine, and the agile, lightweight 6C 1750 of 1929, which many considered Jano's masterpiece.

Development of the 8C 2300 started in 1930 and a year later the car was entered in the Thousand Mile Race as part of the famed *Scuderia*, or "Stable," of Enzo Ferrari, who was then working for Alfa. Contrary to the tradition of the time, it did not win in its debut with Tazio Nuvolari at the wheel, finishing only ninth due to tire problems.

This was a car destined for road racing, but it wasn't limited to that as it could also be produced in small numbers and equipped for day-to-day use; indeed, only about 190 were built up until 1934. According to automotive historian Griffith Borgeson, the car "was sublime in its appearance, design, performance and driving. And, really unsually, even

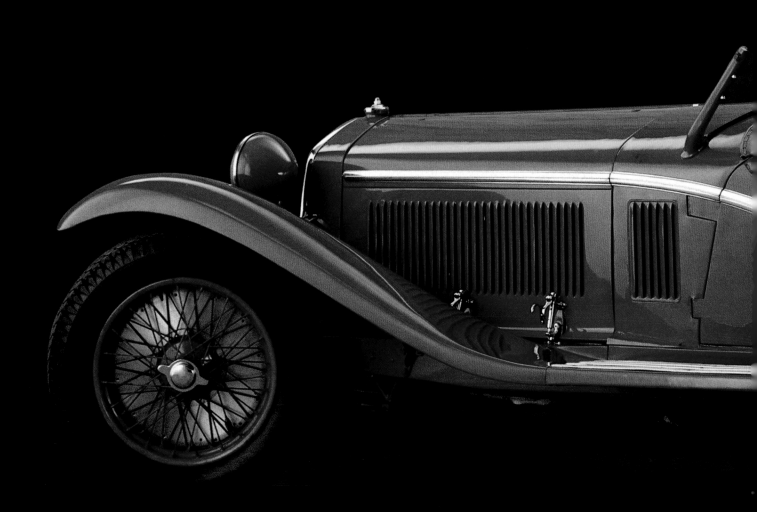

brand with this 8-cylinder Alfa."

Of course, to take one of these cars home required a lot of money. At a time when the average salary of an Italian worker was 450 *lire* per month, and the price of a Fiat Balilla was about 10,000 *lire*, you needed almost 100,000 *lire* for an 8C.

The 8C's unfortunate racing debut was quickly offset by a subsequent victory in the Targa Florio, where Nuvolari managed to navigate Sicilian roads that a thunderstorm had turned into rivers of mud. From there, the racing career of the 8C 2300 was meteoric, with successes in all of the major races of the day, including four consecutive victories at the 24 Hours of Le Mans from 1931 to 1934.

In 1932, *Autocar*, a prestigious British magazine, wrote about the 2300, saying, "The tremendous reserves of power and awesome acceleration can't keep the lid on the incredible resilience of the engine – which even allows you to pick up 9 mph (14 km/h) in fourth – the power of the brakes, or even the superb road holding."

However, in 1934, despite an economic crisis that would have brought Alfa to its knees had the Institute for Industrial Reconstruction not intervened, Jano began work on the 8C 2900 A, an evolution of the 2300 that perhaps was justified by the need to use up thirty extra racing engines. The debut of this car took place at the Mille Miglia in 1936, where it finished first, second and third. The 8C 2900 B, meanwhile, won first and second place in successive

editions of the race in '37 and '38 despite the power of the car being slightly reduced for "civilian use." It would also be victorious in 1947 in the first edition of the Mille Miglia following the Second World War.

Only thirty-six 8C 2900s were produced (six of the A version and thirty of the B), and, as was often done in those days, many were prepared by independent body workers to whom Alfa sold the mechanics and chassis. Among the most noteworthy were the creations of Zagato, Castagna, Pininfarina and those in aluminum by Touring.

For the most part, however, the golden age of the road-ready 8-cylinder Alfa Romeo – the object of desire for kings, princes, maharajas and others among the world's elite – ended with the Second World War.

34-35 The 8C, which was not far off conceptually from the 1929 6C 1750, became famous for its lightness and agility and was considered Vittorio Jano's masterpiece. Its impressive sporting history includes four consecutive wins at Le Mans from 1931 to 1934.

36-37 As often happened in those days, the chassis and engine were assembled by hand at the parent company with body work sourced to outside companies. The Alfa 8C was a highly attractive project to work on, and it pulled in the best names in Italian design: Zagato, Chestnut, Pinin Farina and Touring.

38 top and 38-39 Nuvolari and Guidotti competed in the 1932 Mille Miglia race in an 8C 2300 MM Touring Spider. The 8C, which was sold in both racing and road versions, was very expensive for its time, with a price ten times that of a Fiat Balilla, and was therefore marketed to a wealthy clientele. In fact, it's been said that many Bugatti owners betrayed the French brand to get their hands on one of these Alfas.

38 bottom The main setting for the 8C's success was the Mille Miglia competition, which was held until 1957 and is still considered by many as "the most beautiful race in the world." In the car's 1931 debut, Tazio Nuvolari and Gian Battista Guidotti were forced to undergo several tire changes, which is why they only finished in ninth place.

The new
"alfisti" dream

40 top Produced with extreme attention to detail, the 8C Competizione could nevertheless be customized to customer requirements. It also came with a set of luggage specially made to allow maximum use of the car's scarce interior space. The 8-cylinder engine – which was aligned in a V, unlike its predecessor – and the automatic transmission were derived from Maserati. The price was comparable to that of a Ferrari.

The 8-cylinder engine, now arranged in a V instead of alligned, was used in Alfa's road car production in 1967 thanks to the 33 Stradale, whose name came from its number 33 used in racing. In all, 18 of these cars were produced.

That engine, suitably modified and "civilized," was then reused for the Montreal coupe in 1970 and for a limited run of about 20 of the Alfetta GTV commissioned by a German Alfa importer in 1977. Fans had to wait until the aforementioned 2003 prototype, designed by Wolfgang Egger, to see the glorious 8C name again.

The reviews of this "show car" from fans was enormously positive and Alfa was practically forced to put it into production. The final version was unveiled in 2007, and all of the 500 planned for production were quickly pre-ordered from every part of the world, though mainly from Italy, the United States, Germany and Japan. One was even optioned from Latvia. Sixty percent of the 8C Competizione were requested in the traditional red, reflecting the *Alfisti* need to reconnect to the glorious tradition of the brand.

For a car like this it was not possible to avoid rear-wheel drive, which Alfa had abandoned years earlier. Also, in the absence of other mechanical alternatives, Alfa decided to use the engine and transmission of the Maserati GranTurismo. Aided in part by the lightness of a carbon fiber body, the 8C Competizione's 4.7-liter, 450 hp V8 was a very high performance engine with a maximum speed of around 186 mph (300 km/h).

In the summer of 2005, before production of the 8C Competizione coupe kicked off, Alfa surprisingly introduced the prototype of an 8C roadster at the famous Pebble Beach Concours d'Elegance in California, which left fans clamoring for more. Once again this public acclaim forced Alfa to put the car into another limited production run of 500 between 2009 and 2010.

40-41 and 42-43 The car, presented as a prototype in 2003, went into production in 2007. The 8C for the new millennium had to strongly evoke the Alfa tradition and values. For its design, Wolfgang Egger drew inspiration from the 33 Coupe Stradale and the Giulia TZ, both universally held among the most beautiful Alfa Romeo cars.

44-45 and 45 top In 2005, when nobody knew if the 8C Competizione was going to be built, Alfa introduced a prototype of a surprise 8C Spider at Pebble Beach in California at the Concours d'Elegance, an exhibition devoted to classic cars. The event helped fuel the fire burning in the hearts of fans. Like the coupe version, which supplied the Spider its engine, production was set at 500 units despite the number of requests around the world being much higher. Production took place between 2009 and 2010.

Chrysler Airflow and PT Cruiser

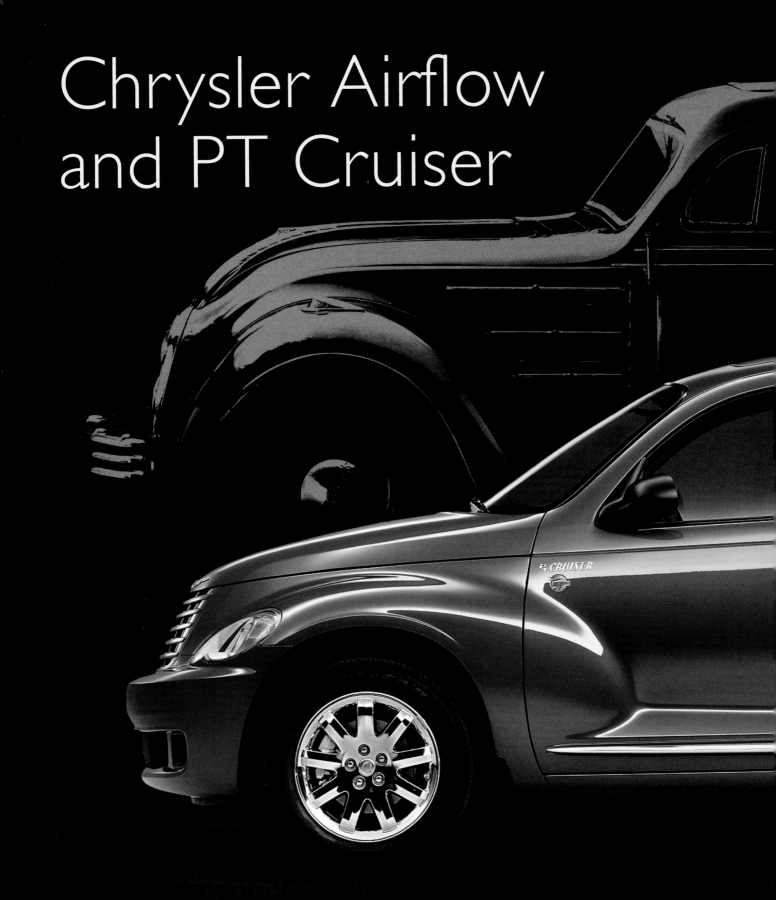

Too modern to be understood

Aerodynamics is a key concept in the automotive field, as it helps reduce the car's air resistance and achieve better performance and fuel consumption. However, it took many years for carmakers to adopt this philosophy. If you exclude the torpedo-shaped prototypes that had no practical use developed early in the last century, the first examples of aerodynamic models date back to 1934: the Czechoslovakian Tatra T77 and the American Chrysler Airflow.

The idea for the Airflow was born in 1927 when Carl Breer, Chrysler's technical director, observed military aircraft in training and decided to apply the same design principles to land vehicles.

It didn't take much for Breer to convince a dreamer like Walter Percy Chrysler, who founded the company in 1924, of the idea's merit, and he immediately received the means to put it in practice. The most important of these were a wind tunnel and the expert advice of Orville Wright, the man who, with his brother Wilbur, had first flown an airplane in 1903.

The revolutionary design of the Airflow was characterized by the partially streamlined rear wheels, headlights integrated into the fender and a radiator grill that followed the curve of the hood.

The interior, meanwhile, was large. To gain extra inches the engine was moved forward so that both rows of seats were placed between the front and rear wheels. Before this, passengers seated in the back were usually located above the rear wheels. Also, doors were lowered to make the car more accessible. These innovations allowed a perfect distribution of weight at full load, which promoted stability on slippery surfaces.

48-49 The 8-cylinder, 5300 cc, 122 hp engine, combined with a 3-speed manual transmission, was able to bring the car to a top speed of 90 mph (150 km/h). But it was more than its performance that got people talking about the Airflow. It was its futuristic design that really turned heads.

49 top *A hood hinged to the windshield base, with the opening at the front, is now used by almost all cars. When the Airflow debuted on the market, however, this approach was considered innovative.*

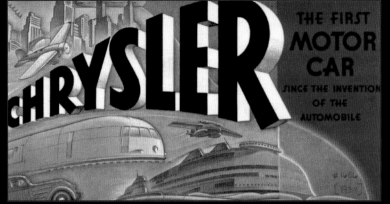

CHRYSLER

THE FIRST
MOTOR
CAR
SINCE THE INVENTION
OF THE
AUTOMOBILE

Chrysler was at its peak from 1936 to 1949 and was only behind the giant General Motors in the number of cars registered in the United States.

50 top The Airflow proved a commercial flop. Nevertheless, Chrysler was at its peak from 1936 to 1949 and was only behind the giant General Motors in the number of cars registered in the United States.

50-51 Through a series of aerodynamic innovations, Carl Breer, the designer of the Airflow, managed to develop a car that provided 40 percent less resistance to air than competitive models.

Security was held in high regard. At a time when rivals General Motors and Ford were still incorporating wood parts for the frame, Chrysler responded with a structure made entirely of steel. To demonstrate this robustness, an advertisement played in theaters showed an Airflow being thrown from a 100-foot (34 m) high cliff and then continuing to drive.

In 1934, on the 10th anniversary of the company, everything was ready for launch. The Airflow, available in either a four-door or two-door coupe version, was presented at the New York Auto Show and put on the market under two different brands: the more luxurious Chrysler, with an 8-cylinder engine, and the spartan De Soto, which had 6 cylinders.

The car, however, proved to be a fiasco, and not just because of its design, which was considered too futuristic for the time. The main problem was the poor quality of the first 3000 cars produced. For example, the engine would fall off its supports when you exceeded 80 mph (130 km/h).

Despite the growth of the U.S. market following the Great Depression, Chrysler's sales fell, though the De Soto suffered more since all it had was the Airflow. In 1935, Chrysler tried to remedy the situation with the launch of the Airstream, which had an aerodynamic appearance but a much more traditional design which better met the taste of the public. The strategy paid off. For every Airflow produced, four Airstreams were assembled.

The Airflow's adventure ended in 1937 after an unspectacular four-year career and less than 30,000 units sold. In the following decades, however, all the other carmakers began focusing on aerodynamics. The first to achieve success with it was the Peugeot 402 in 1938.

Fiat 500

Small in size but large in numbers

58 top *The picture shows a moment in the production of the 500 Topolino (Italian for Mickey Mouse) in the late 1940s. The car was developed in 1936 at the request of Benito Mussolini, who wanted a car that would help motorize Italy, just as Adolf Hitler was doing in Germany with the Beetle.*

When you consider the impact of the car on Italian history, one name more than any other stands above the rest: the Fiat 500.

To be precise, there have been four generations of the Fiat 500. The 500 of 1936, better known as "Topolino," was the first compact car in the world to be produced in large quantities. The "true" 500, however, the one that remains in the collective imagination and is the focus here, is the version created in 1957. In all, 3.7 million were produced, and the "true" 500 became a major influence in the motorization of Italy.

Between 1991 and 1998, the story took a slight detour with the Cinquecento (Italian for "five hundred"), but in 2007 the 500 returned, inspired by the glory of generations past but with a totally different approach to dimensions and mechanics.

The "Topolino" 500 of the '30s was decidedly no-frills and low-cost compared to its sisters in the Fiat product line, but at that time cars were still a luxury few could afford.

That would change, however, after the Second World War, partly because of the Suez Crisis, which raised the cost of oil and sparked demand for more economical cars. In 1953, the Deutsche Fiat company pitched Turin the idea of a relatively spartan car that was practically a cross between a motorcycle and an automobile with a rear engine. Dante Giacosa, Fiat's legendary technical director, considered the proposal and decided to develop it according to his own ideas, some of which were already being used for the 600. The prototype 110, as it was classified internally, was presented to Fiat management at the end of 1955 and was immediately approved with enthusiasm. In less than two years the new 500 was born, with "new" serving to distance itself from the old "Topolino."

However, this "egg" on four wheels was almost too bare bones: it had no rear seats, no windows that opened, no defogging windshield system and no chrome, plus it barely exceeded 50 mph (80 km/h). Basically, it lacked anything that could titillate a society that had already begun dreaming of the good life. In fact, even the price wasn't very alluring. The new 500 cost 490,000 *lire*, which was relatively high when you consider that the much faster and more attractive Fiat 600 cost only 590,000 *lire*.

58-59 *Versions A and B, characterized by a vertical grill and external headlights, allowed the 500 to survive wartime. The profoundly modernized Type C appeared in 1949 with a horizontal grill and embedded headlights. It was manufactured until 1955.*

Accordingly, reception for the 500 was lukewarm, so much so that only three months later Fiat took action, increasing the 579 cc engine by 13 to 15 hp and improving the offer. The new "normal" 500 was the same price but came equipped with a richer array of features. Meanwhile, the "economic" 500 was almost as bare bones as the original but cost 25,000 *lire* less. Furthermore, for those who had bought the car months earlier Fiat offered a refund for the difference in price or a free retooling that would bring the standard version up to date with the newer models. These emergency tactics helped launch a long career, one characterized by only a few changes, which would make the 500 the uncontested queen of the compact cars.

In 1958, Fiat produced the Sport version. Powered by a new 21 hp engine, the Sport model had a half canvas, half metal roof that could be opened at the front and was slightly elevated at the back to make the rear passenger seats more comfortable. These changes put into practice the classical configuration that characterizes the 500 and which would be used until the end of its commercial life. The only exception was a change in the opening system of the doors, which were front-hinged starting in 1965. Also in '65, the company dropped the "New" from the name, reverting simply to "500."

The car remained in production until 1975, when it made way for the 126, which had appeared three years earlier. However, the Giardiniera station wagon, which had been released in 1960, remained on the market until 1977, albeit under the name Autobianchi.

The 500 is deeply rooted in Italian culture. In fact, there are few films shot in Italy in the '60s and '70s where the car doesn't appear, and it made more than just a mere appearance is movies like *The Motorized* (1961), *Caprice Italian Style* (1965), *I Knew Her Well* (1965), *We All Loved Each Other So Much* (1974) and *One Hundred Steps* (2000). In 2001, it also played an important role in the road movie called, appropriately, *500!*. And, of course, the 500 comes up in an almost unlimited amount of technical literature. The car's impact is such that it is often used as something of an Italian ambassador in various events. During the 2009 Christmas holiday, three 500s left from Bolzano, having collected children's letters to Santa Claus in various countries across Europe, and then delivered them to Rovaniemi, the fabled residence of Saint Nick.

Although, from a commercial point of view, the car is predominately an Italian phenomenon, the echoes of success have gone much further. The car has a prominent role in the Japanese cartoon series *Lupin III*, the Disney animated movie *Cars* (2006) and the video game *Gran Turismo 4*, where it is featured alongside supercars of much higher stature.

60 The Topolino 500 was not exactly cheap. The price was equivalent to about 20 times the average salary of a skilled worker. Those who could afford it didn't just use it as a "toy car," as shown by this model towing a Dragonfly trailer.

60-61 Even though it did not have the great success of the Beetle, the Topolino has the distinction of being the first economy car in automotive history to be mass-produced. Close to 600,000 cars were produced in a span of nearly 19 years, including the period of the Second World War.

62 top The New 500 ("New" served to distinguish it from the
Topolino 500) was presented in 1956 and remained in production
until 1975, with 3,700,000 cars produced. This version, more than
any other, was the one that helped motorize Italy. For many it
became the family car despite its small size and modest livability.
The rear seats were sufficient to accommodate two children and
the trunk had a very limited capacity, but this didn't prevent it
from being used on road trips, a fact that seems incredible
considering our modern travel habits.

62-63 *The last version of the 500 with the R (short for Rinnovata) name was produced for three years alongside the 126, which was replaced in 1975. Surviving the 126's demise was the station wagon version, which continued to be produced until 1977 under the Autobianchi name.*

63 *This drawing shows some of the different versions of the 500 sedan. There were also luxury and sports varieties sold by specialists such as Moretti and Giannini and countless special editions manufactured throughout Italy.*

64-65 *Due to its enormous and rapid success, the 500 quickly became a cultural phenomenon, one that soon even influenced the fashion world, as evidenced by this unusual parade of cars and clothes on September 24, 1968, at the Place de la Concorde in Paris.*

1957 « NUOVA 500 » transformable 1" et 2e série

1958 « 500 Sport »

1959 « NUOVA 500 » toit ouvrant

1960 « 500 D »

1965 « 500 F »

1968 « 500 L »

From its predecessor, the 500 of the '90s took very little. It had a front engine and a boxy body that was unattractive, partly due to its inability to match small external dimensions with interior roominess. To keep production costs down, the car had to be built in Russia and then, eventually, in Poland, where the production lines of the 126 had already been moved. The '90s version had disc brakes, a hatchback and optional air conditioning, but it never managed to work its way into the hearts of motorists, some of whom believed it had usurped a name filled with meaning and history without ever possessing the same charisma.

The 500 was produced from 1991 to 1998, when it was restyled and renamed the 600, partly to play with another historical similarity.

At the beginning of the 21st century – inspired by the nostalgia wave brought on by the VW New Beetle, the Chrysler PT Cruiser and, above all, BMW's MINI – Fiat decided it was time to resurrect the 500 but in a more intriguing manner than in 1991. This time, they decided to use a body and interior that shared features of the "true" 500 but used the modern mechanics (that of the Panda) that were totally different from the original. To further increase the ties to the original, the revamped 500 was unveiled on July 4, 2007, exactly 50 years after the launch of its illustrious forerunner.

The 500 of today is far bulkier, sophisticated and refined in its mechanics, with rich features and performance; the Abarth, for example, can exceed 125 mph (200 km/h). No longer a model for the masses, the new 500 is a flirtatious and expensive car sure to please the image-consious.

Everyone's sweetheart

66-67 *The sliding canvas sunroof was one of the distinct characteristics of the first 500. When Fiat decided to revive its most famous model in 2007 it took this feature into account and, in the spring of 2009, presented the 500 C (for "convertible") with the same roof opening method, even if it was now electronically operated.*

68-69 The 500 of today is mechanically very different from that of 1957. It has front-wheel drive and a front engine, but the style remains quite faithful to the original. In fact, because it so closely conjures up the past, it's Fiat's weapon of choice for its return to the U.S. market, where it's hoped the car will become an icon, like it is in Europe.

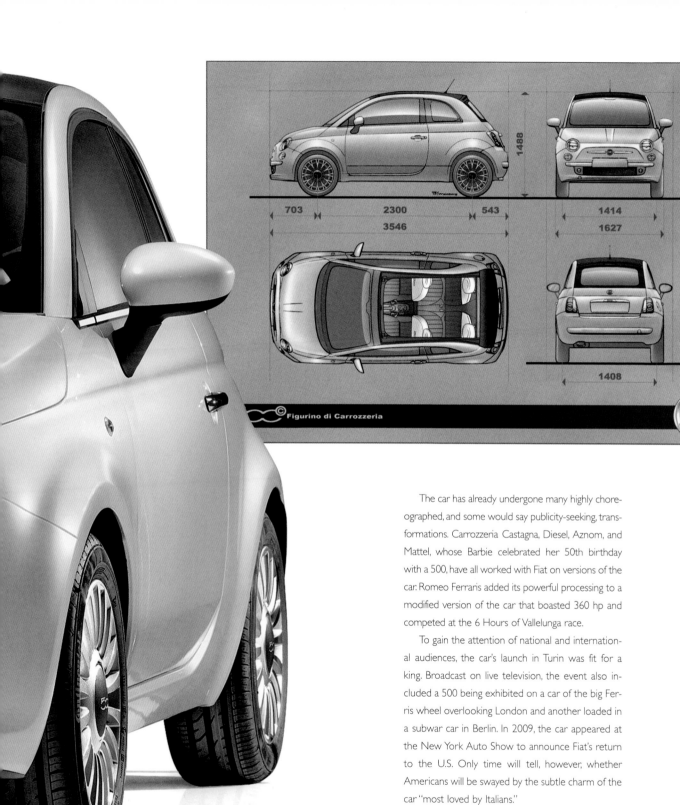

1488

703   2300   543
3546

1414
1627

1408

©Figurino di Carrozzeria

FIAT

The car has already undergone many highly chore-ographed, and some would say publicity-seeking, trans-formations. Carrozzeria Castagna, Diesel, Aznom, and Mattel, whose Barbie celebrated her 50th birthday with a 500, have all worked with Fiat on versions of the car. Romeo Ferraris added its powerful processing to a modified version of the car that boasted 360 hp and competed at the 6 Hours of Vallelunga race.

To gain the attention of national and internation-al audiences, the car's launch in Turin was fit for a king. Broadcast on live television, the event also in-cluded a 500 being exhibited on a car of the big Fer-ris wheel overlooking London and another loaded in a subwar car in Berlin. In 2009, the car appeared at the New York Auto Show to announce Fiat's return to the U.S. Only time will tell, however, whether Americans will be swayed by the subtle charm of the car "most loved by Italians."

69 Even the dimensions are quite different from the old 500, which was less than 10 feet (3 meters) long and weighed less than 1500 pounds (700 kg). But the car of today is no spartan, super economy car but a compact sedan that wants to be trendy, following the path blazed by the new MINI.

Volkswagen Beetle and New Beetle

The German revolution

The hum of the air-cooled boxer engine was once the soundtrack of the German economic miracle. Strangely enough, the car designed by Ferdinand Porsche at the behest of Hitler might never have succeeded without the determination of the English Army. But let's start from the beginning.

The year was 1934 when the Führer announced plans for a car of the people, or "Volks-Wagen." In 1936, the prototypes for these cars, which had rear engines and rear-wheel drive, underwent their first tests, and already the characteristic Beetle look was taking shape. According to Hitler himself, the car was to be called the KDF Wagen ("Kraft Durch Freude," meaning "strength through joy"). The name might have been terrible, but the technical innovations adopted by designers and manufacturers left everyone who saw it in awe, especially considering the announced price of only 1000 marks.

Some saw more than a hint of the Tatra V570, designed by Hans Ledwinka in Czechoslovakia in 1933, in the Beetle, but that didn't alter the significant impact of the German car. Its light alloy engine, four wheel independent suspension and automatic choke, among other innovations, were all far ahead of their time. In 1939, the KDF Wagen made its debut, but due to the outbreak of the Second World War civilian production was taken over by the military. "Uniformed" versions of the car were made famous in countless wartime movies, and the Beetle was honored with the names Kommandeurwagen, Kübelwagen and, in the case of the amphibious version, Schwimmwagen. After the war, however, the Volkswagen factory was on its knees.

At that point, the English Army sent Major Ivan Hirst to the factory in Wolfsburg. Hirst was told that, "It's sufficient that somebody's residing over it, so just sit there, that's enough." But the 29-year-old official came to the conclusion that the machines had for the most part been salvaged and that they could re-start production of vehicles for the Queen's armed forces. After testing a prototype, his superiors signed an order for 20,000 cars.

Volkswagen was back in business, despite the fact that the damaged roof of the factory was still being repaired with tree branches and tarpaulin. Production, however, did not take off as expected, and the project only went ahead because of the stubbornness of Hirst, who placed the first 56 cars produced in the Netherlands. Shipments to Belgium, Denmark, Luxembourg, Sweden and Switzerland followed. With them came the reborn company's first hard currency: 21 million marks, the result of 4464 Beetles sold in 1948.

In 1949, the factory was handed back to the Germans and put in the hands of director Heinrich Nordhoff, who declared, "The Beetle has as many drawbacks as there are fleas on a dog." Nevertheless, the funny little car almost single-handedly motorized Germany thanks to its stubborn reliability. By 1950 the company had produced 100,000 cars. Three years later, the total was 500,000. This staggering growth accounted for 42.5% of Germany's total car market and continued unabated, so much so that the millionth Beetle, a gold car that had its chrome outfitted with precious stones, was produced in 1955.

72 top The sketch of the future Volkswagen Beetle was drawn by
Adolf Hitler in Monaco during the summer of 1932. The dictator
brought the project forward, hoping it would motorize Germany. The
famous Autobahn highways branched across the nation were also built.

72-73 Hitler speaks from the podium during a ceremony laying
the cornerstone of the Volkswagen manufacturing plant in the city
of Wolfsburg. Before him are a few prototypes of the Beetle,
including a convertible version.

74 top Ferdinand Porsche, left, discusses the design of the Beetle with his son Ferry. It is no coincidence that the first Porsche, called the 356, shared many technical innovations with Volkswagen, starting with the boxer engine.

74-75 Although the design and development phase was initiated before the outbreak of the Second World War, the road version of the car went into production only after the conflict, ten years after Hitler's original prediction.

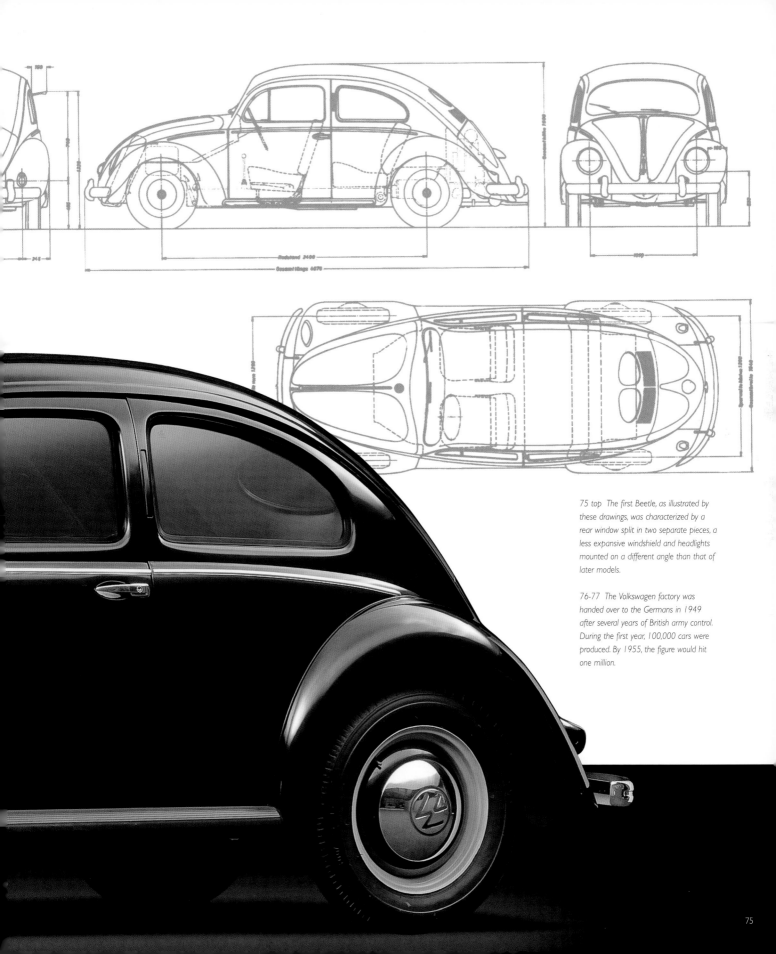

75 top The first Beetle, as illustrated by these drawings, was characterized by a rear window split in two separate pieces, a less expansive windshield and headlights mounted on a different angle than that of later models.

76-77 The Volkswagen factory was handed over to the Germans in 1949 after several years of British army control. During the first year, 100,000 cars were produced. By 1955, the figure would hit one million.

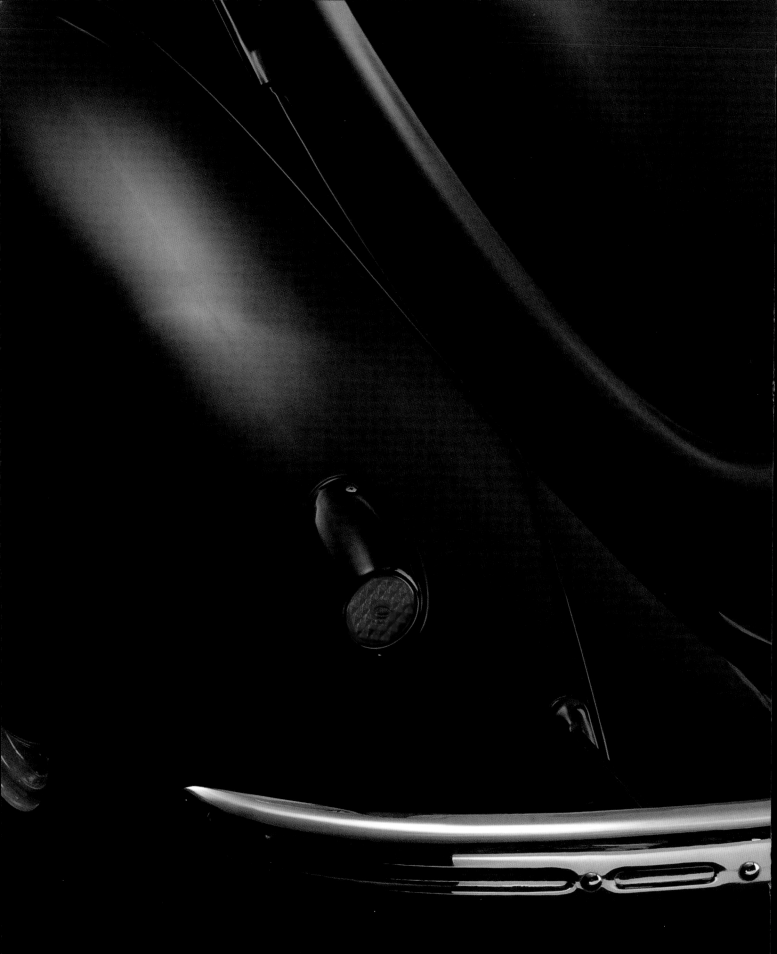

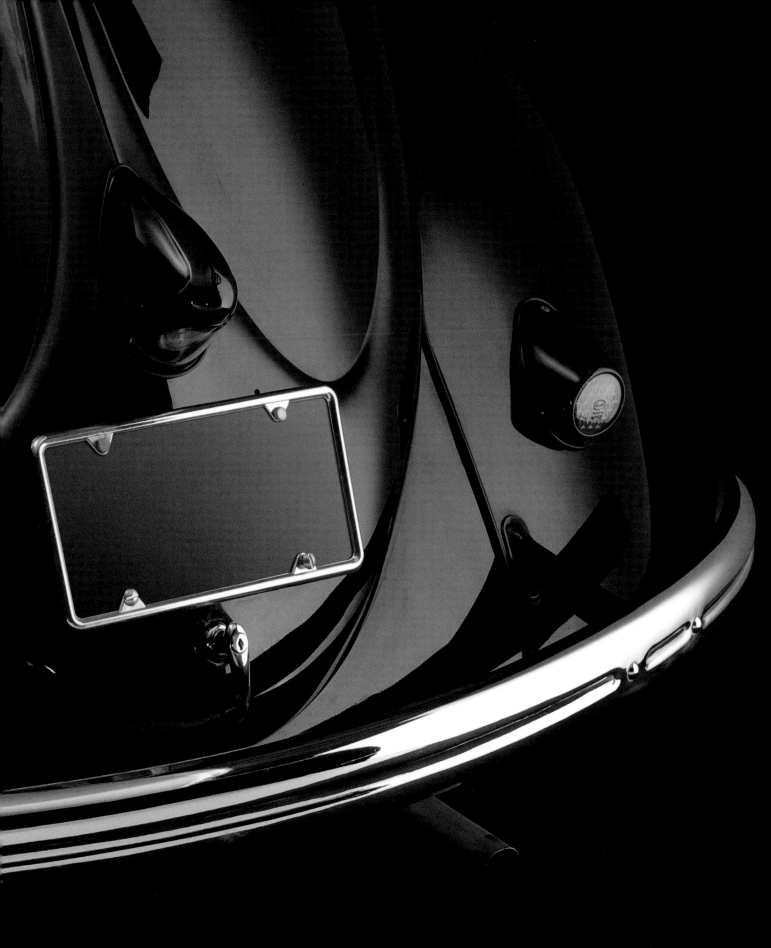

78 top A billboard of the 1950s. Ever since its release, the Beetle has enjoyed many great publicity campaigns which have often been based on irony. One of the most popular was "Air never boils," a message that underlined the reliability of the car's air-cooled engines and poked fun at the water-based systems used by its competitors.

78 bottom A Volkswagen worker poses in Wolfsburg in front of a Beetle with a miniature Model T Ford in his hand. On February 17, 1972, the Beetle broke the American car's production record of 15,007,033 units produced.

78-79 The German freighter Ravenstein has just finished unloading a Volkswagen shipment on the pier in Baltimore on March 11, 1956. The Beetle has always been highly acclaimed in the U.S. market, so much so that to meet customer needs production of the car started in Mexico.

30 A worker controls the immersion of the bodywork in a color
bath. By 1965 there were five production facilities for the car in
Germany and together they churned out a total of one million
Beetles a year.

There were five factories by 1965 – Hannover, Kassel, Braunschweig, Emden and the original in Wolfsburg – producing one million cars a year. Improvements were so continuous that if you compared a car to one from the first generation, you'd find that 5002 of the total 5008 components had been changed.

With time, the split rear window disappeared and the windows became increasingly larger, among many other changes. The car's proverbial strength and spirit, however, were never less democratic. Anyone, regardless of social status or income, could own one.

The "lifting" of 1967 did not alter this essence. The headlights were now rounder and more vertical, the bumpers more square and wraparound and the taillights were larger and more powerful, as the electrical system was upgraded from 6 to 12 volts. But the car remained as unique as ever.

Not even the arrival of the '70s-era Beetle could change the car's appeal. The newcomer had a more rounded front end, a more sophisticated front suspension and was generally more compact in order to free up space for luggage. Eventually, even a curved windshield and a new dashboard were integrated.

The fairytale, however, had begun to end, even if on February 17, 1972, the assembly line turned out Beetle number 15,007,034, a total that exceeded the Model T Ford, which had been the best-selling car in history. After only two more years, in fact, production was suspended in Wolfsburg, which had become known as "The City of the Beetle" and whose factory alone had built almost 12 million Beetles, to make room for the Golf.

In 1978, production in Europe ceased, although the convertible remained on European assembly lines for another two years. Models sold in Europe from then on came from Mexican factories in Puebla, where the twenty millionth Beetle was produced in May 1981. This is also where the last model ever (number 21,529,464) was produced on July 31, 2003. As part of the special "Ultima Edición" series, the final car was blue, sported floral decorations in the colors of the Mexican flag and was powered by a 1600 cc engine and 44 hp, the last hurrah of the four-cylinder boxer derived from the first prototype, which had 700 cc and 22.5 hp.

80-81 The Beetle has always remained true to itself. The main changes, brought on by requirements and standards in some countries, included headlights that were more vertical and effective, turn signals on models destined for the U.S. and were later standard on all models from the 1970s on, and a more enveloping bumper.

Beetle-mania wasn't exclusive to Europe, however, as even the United States fell victim to the car's spell. In 1963 there were waiting lists of up to five months to get one. Meanwhile, the Beetle also had a career as an actress. In 1969, Disney produced the film *Herbie The Love Bug*, which revolved around a car with human feelings capable of beating real sports cars in races.

The film was a huge success and there were many sequels: *Herbie Rides Again* (1974), *Herbie Goes to Monte Carlo* (1977), *Herbie Goes Bananas* (1980) and *Herbie: Fully Loaded* (2005), not to mention the 1982 TV series *Herbie The Matchmaker* and the 1997 TV movie *Herbie: The Love Bug*.

82 The Love Bug was a 1969 film by Robert Stevenson that was a huge box office success and sparked a long series of sequels.

82-83 The film series that started with The Love Bug *is full of spectacular scenes, breathtaking chases and comic situations. In addition to the five feature films, there was also a television series and made-for-TV movie.*

Echoes of glory

In 1994, Volkswagen took the prototype of the Concept 1 to the Detroit Auto Show. The design for this car, developed in the California style of Simi Valley, was clearly inspired by the original Beetle, which at that time was still in production in Mexico. The reception in Detroit was triumphant, and soon after a convertible version was presented at the Geneva Auto Show. The production model, called the New Beetle, was put on the market in 1998.

Despite the design, however, the New Beetle was also built in Puebla and had little to do with its progenitor. In fact, it was based on the mechanics of the Golf, with a front engine and front-wheel drive. The Golf, though, had much more space for passengers and luggage.

In addition, the price of the New Beetle was high and the engine was rather undersized and lacking. Sales were decent in the U.S., while in Europe the car received little attention, to the point that by its

10th anniversary in 2008 only one million New Beetles had been produced in total.

In an effort to revive sales, a convertible version was released in 2003, and in 2005 upgrades and changes were made to the design and engine.

Nevertheless, at the 2009 Los Angeles Auto Show, the "Final Edition" was presented, which ended the career of the heir to the legendary Beetle, the car that more than any other has helped create the image of the reliable German car.

84 For many motorists, the Beetle embodied the spirit of freedom. It was used for road trips and adventures of all kinds, despite the limitations of a small cargo space and tight interior, especially for rear passengers.

85 Despite the obvious resemblance to the original Beetle, the New Beetle born at the end of the 1990s did not win the hearts of fans the way Volkswagen had hoped. In fact, its career only lasted 12 years, a modest number compared with the more than 50 years racked up by the original. In the U.S., however, it had considerably better luck, especially the convertible version which, like its ancestor, had a fabric roof that remained visible even when folded.

86-87 *One of the criticisms of the New Beetle was that it was as large as a Golf but had less space for cargo and passengers. It was also expensive, something that put it in stark contrast with one of the features upon which the Beetle had built its legend: affordability.*

88-89 *The New Beetle has always had a soul that stretched outside Europe. It was, after all, designed by Volkswagen's California design center and it continues to be produced in Puebla, Mexico, where production of the original Beetle continued until 2003.*

The celebrity of war

Cars don't have feelings but they're perfectly capable of evoking emotion. Two of the most common are joy and pride, but in the case of the Jeep you can add gratitude. According to General George Marshall, the Jeep was the largest American contribution to modern warfare. For Dwight Eisenhower, Supreme Comander of the Allied forces in Europe and later the U.S. president, it was one of three important tools, in addition to the Dakota transport aircraft and landing craft, that won the war. If you agree, you might want to thank a Jeep the next time you see one.

By 1935, the U.S. military wanted a light vehicle, and the outbreak of war forced the U.S. Army to hasten its efforts. On July 11, 1940, a military commission determined the specifications for a 4x4 reconnaissance vehicle. Interested factories had to submit a request for participation within 11 days, produce a prototype within 49 days and build 70 working models in 75 days.

Only three carmakers accepted the challenge: American Bantam, Ford and Willys-Overland. Despite the fact that Willys had submitted the most economical option, the contract was won by Bantam, the only participant able to meet the delivery times.

Because the company was small, however, it alone could not meet the demands of the War Department. Its design plans were soon revealed to both Ford and Willys-Overland, both of whom readily assembled as many similar models as possible. The final products from all three – Bantam BRC-40, Willys MA and Ford GP – were eventually approved and 1500 of each were ordered. In July 1941, however, a fresh supply of 16,000 vehicles was needed and the Willys version was chosen because of its more powerful engine and the fact that it cost less to design and produce. Thus, the MB was born. However, it had to be accompanied by a version produced under license from Ford (the GPW) to reach the number of vehicles requested. Meanwhile, Bantam, which had produced the original idea, had to be content with a contract for the production of trailers.

92-93 The original Willys MB performed in the Second World War with a 2200 cc, 61 hp gasoline engine, which did not permit the best road handling or performance. The maximum speed on asphalt barely exceeded 60 mph (100 km/h). But the important thing was for the car to go everywhere and seem indestructible, and those goals were achieved in full.

There are several theories for the origin of the name "Jeep." The most accepted is that it came from the pronunciation of the initials GP, which stood for "General Purpose" (or "multi-purpose") and distinguished this category of vehicles.

Early models were very rustic. They had a parallelepiped-shaped hood, a cockpit protected by side rails and a folding windshield. To reduce the consumption of steel, which in wartime is needed more in heavy industry, there was an idea to make the body out of plywood. However, the desire to protect the soldiers on board prevailed and the project was aborted.

The Jeep truly went everywhere. During an unveiling, a fully-loaded Willys scaled the steps of the Capitol in Washington, D.C. On some models built for the European front, tires were replaced by railway wheels to travel on the tracks.

By the end of the war, 639,245 had left the assembly line, destined for every Allied army. Fifty-six percent of these versatile vehicles carried the Willys brand. But this wasn't the end, thanks to the Korean War and numerous requests from armies around the world. There was an evolution of the MB, the M38, which was built from 1950 to 1957.

That marked the end of the car's military history, but a version built for the general public continues its career to this day.

It was in 1945 that the first CJ, or "Civilian Jeep," which used the MB's platform, was put on the market, and since then many developments and updates have followed. The 2A lasted until 1949 and the 3A until 1953, but the most famous was undoubtedly the 3B, produced from 1953 to 1968. Its design was sold under license to foreign manufacturers such as Mitsubishi, which made a version until 1998, and Mahindra, whose version is still found in some markets.

The CJ-5 (1954–1983) brought a richer and more powerful engine range, with the adoption of 6- and 8-cylinder units as well as the 4-cylinder that had characterized the car from the beginning. The CJ-6 name was used for an underappreciated pick-up. The CJ-7 (1976–1986) offered more interior space, thanks to a longer wheelbase, and modern touches such as an optional automatic transmission and a new permanent four-wheel drive system called Quadra-Trac. The names CJ-8 (1981–1986) and CJ-10 (1981–1985) were used only for the pick-up.

WHEN THE GOING IS TOUGH, when you have a heavy load to pull, the Universal "Jeep's" 4-wheel drive puts amazing tractive power at your command. That's why the "Jeep" can haul supplies through mud and snow . . . take workers across roadless countrysides . . . pull almost any farm implement. The front drive-axle of the "Jeep" is a "business end" that broadens the utility of this versatile vehicle for industry and the farm.

THE 'JEEP' HAS TWO 'BUSINESS ENDS'

2 or 4 Wheel Drive, Plus Power Take-off, for Widest Utility

FOR ECONOMICAL POWER . . . FOR ALL-AROUND VERSATILITY

GET A 'Jeep'

94-95 The Jeep was rather contained in size but was nevertheless heavier than the German army car, the Kubelwagen, which was born from the original Beetle project. The Wyllis also was more mobile and had excellent off-road performance.

95 In 1946, a year after the end of World War II, Jeep advertisements began to appear. These ads listed the vehicle's benefits for farmers and anyone who wanted to use it for civilian purposes. The Jeep's commercial life had begun.

The 4x4 icon

The limits of the CJ project, however, began to emerge in the '80s, so the Wrangler was introduced in 1987. It had a longer wheelbase, wider windshield and lowered body, which meant lower ground clearance. The overall style did not undergo major changes and some body parts were even interchangeable with the previous generation. But the appearance of the rectangular front headlights in place of the traditional round lights sparked an uproar among fans. The engines were a 2.5-liter 4-cylinder and a 4-liter 6-cylinder with solid performance but downright embarrassing fuel consumption. The Wrangler got only 16 miles (25 km) with one gallon (4 liters) of gasoline if you drove with a light foot.

The TJ generation (1996–2006) returned the round headlights, to the delight of fans, and adopted the more sophisticated and effective suspension of its big sister, the Grand Cherokee.

In 2007, the JK version made its appearance and sported numerous changes, including a larger body and a completely revised yet traditional design. A five-door configuration and a turbo diesel engine that met the demands of European drivers were also available.

The desire to adapt this icon of the past to the present is evident, even if the formula stays spartan in spirit. Recently, the car has been enriched by modern electronic devices, and in 2008 a hybrid prototype was even unveiled with a combination gasoline/electric engine.

Now the car is in the hands of Fiat. The ups and downs of Willys-Overland have seen the company change its name to the Jeep Corporation before merging with American Motors, which in turn was absorbed by Chrysler in 1987.

96-97 *The 65th anniversary Jeep Wrangler was created in 2006 to celebrate the legendary 4x4's history. The car was characterized by fenders colored the same as the body instead of the traditional black, graphite alloy wheels, a silver dashboard and a two-tone interior finish.*

97 *The first Wrangler in history to have rear doors, the Unlimited, was presented at the 2006 New York Auto Show. The car's wheelbase increased by 17 inches (43 cm), which produced much more interior space for passengers and cargo.*

98-99 *The latest generation of the Wrangler, dubbed the JK, comes equipped with a 6-cylinder, 200 hp gasoline engine. To meet the demands of the European market, a 4-cylinder, 177 hp turbo diesel inherited from its big sister, the Cherokee, was also made available.*

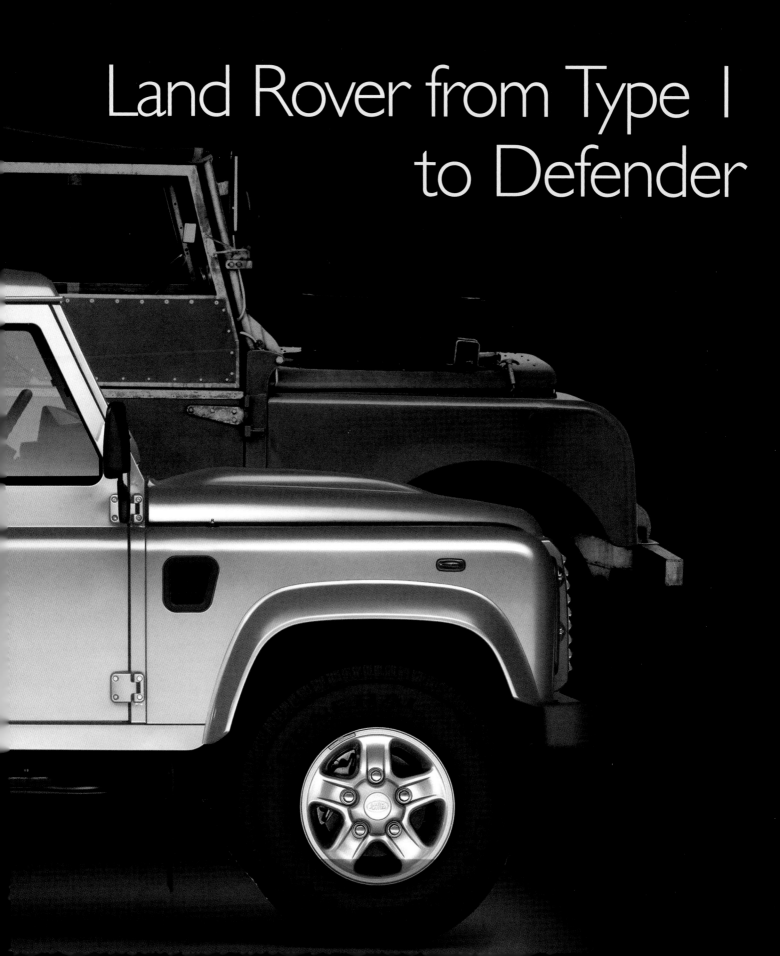

Land Rover from Type I to Defender

"Durability was based on drivers' discomfort — we damaged more drivers then vehicles during testing." This phrase, attributed to one of the designers of the first Land Rover, summarizes the type of vehicle that the British company wanted to achieve: hard, pure, indestructible and unstoppable.

If the Jeep was born from the demands of war, the Land Rover owes its existence to the exceptional severity of the 1947 English winter. The estate of the Wilks family, which controlled Rover, had been covered by storm-battered trees and the cars of the household were not well suited to remove them. This forced chief engineer Maurice Wilks to buy a surplus military Caterpillar for the job.

For some time, Maurice had noticed that his neighbor, Colonel Nash, had a Willys Jeep, which Maurice managed to acquire in exchange for his tree-removing Caterpillar. When his brother, Spencer Wilks, who was the principal owner of Rover, went to see Maurice, he was impressed by the Jeep. Since spare parts were hard to find, both men were worried about what would happen if the car broke down. The solution was obvious — they needed to build an equivalent English version.

The first such prototype did not even have a name and used a weak 1400 cc, 48 hp engine mounted on an American frame with green paint taken from Royal Air Force aircraft used during the Second World War. Moreover, the rationing of steel, which was given only to those who produced cars for export, forced the Wilks to fall back on aluminum. This hindrance turned out to be quite useful, since aluminum is light and invulnerable to rust, and helped to create the reputation of the "stain-less" English 4WD. The hardships of the postwar period also influenced the shape of the car. A lack of resources made it impossible to buy the presses suitable for shaping metal, forcing the use of straight and rectangular elements.

Originally, the driver's seat was in a central position, not only because this allowed the car to be used in all markets, without having to provide both right- and left-hand traffic-ready cars, but also because it allowed access to tax breaks that the British government granted for agricultural machinery. This wasn't a complete stretch since initially this off-roader was used primarily by farmers thanks to a government order that allowed the operation of machines needed to work the fields.

At the end of testing, the only thing missing was a name. Ultimately, adding "Land" to Rover was the easiest and most natural choice. Legend has it that the inspiration for the logo came from the oval shape of the sardine tins the Wilks brothers ate from while testing the early prototypes.

The Land Rover Type 1 made its debut at the 1948 Amsterdam Auto Show. Compared to the prototype, this model came with a 1600 cc, 50 hp engine and square-shaped front fenders. The company justified this choice by saying, "Born this way because of our inability to shape aluminum, the fenders will remain because you can rest a cup of tea on them."

The car's success exceeded expectations and orders came from around the world. Land Rovers were used by soldiers and farmers, public figures like Winston Churchill and Queen Elizabeth II and, above all, by explorers and adventurers all over the globe.

102 top *Habib Bourguiba, the founder and first president of modern Tunisia after its independence from France, rides atop a Land Rover on June 1, 1955, upon his return from exile.*

102-103 *The first generation Land Rover didn't provide vents in the front grill to correspond with the headlights until after 1951. The model seen here is so basic that it does not even have handles on its doors.*

In 1955, three university students went from London to Singapore, a trip that was later duplicated by the carmaker. There were countless adventures of this kind, which brought the car publicity but also helped to improve the product.

In 1951, the headlights were moved from inside the radiator grill to its outer edges. The engine was increased to 2 liters, with a curious semi-permanent integrated drive system changed to the more tradi-

tional four-wheel drive solution. The car's length was also increased, from 80 to 86 inches (200 to 220 cm). A stretch version, nicknamed "107" for its length in inches, was proposed. In 1957, the diesel version debuted.

The Type II arrived ten years later. The gasoline engine was increased to 2200 cc and 77 hp while the body underwent slight improvements and was also enlarged. The Land Rover also was being pro-

duced under license in Spain by a company called Santa Ana under the name Santana, an arrangement which continues to this day.

A downturn hit the British car industry in the late 1960s and major brands merged to form the British Leyland Motor Corporation, or BLMC. Land Rover resisted and 1971 defiantly presented the Range Rover, the first luxury SUV, and the Land Rover Type III. Aesthetically, the latter was recog-

nizable by headlights positioned on the fender and not inserted into the grill, although in reality this change had already been implemented in some countries in accordance with different road safety standards. Also, the grill was made out of plastic and not steel. Farmers felt this last change the most because they often used the steel grill as a barbecue in the fields.

The interior, meanwhile, featured improved er-gonomic controls and equipment. The oil crisis also brought forth a need for longer gears, which improved fuel economy and handling on asphalt.

The Type III was the official car of the 1983 Camel Trophy, the most grueling and challenging competition for off-road vehicles, held in Zaire. This occasion was also used to test innovations which led to new modifications, including a permanent four-wheel drive system and the use of the Range Rover's suspension. These additions precipitated a name change, with the car now called the 85 (which was called the 90 starting in 1985) and the 110, the numbers again indicating the length of the car in inches.

The Land Rover 90 and 110 were the official cars of the Camel Trophy in 1984 (Brazil), 1985 (Borneo), 1986 (Australia), 1988 (Sulawesi, Indonesia) and 1989 (Amazon).

The everlasting workhorse

in 1990, the original Land Rover Name, which had become a recognizable brand, was abandoned in favor of Defender, which is used today.

In 2007, Ford, which owned Land Rover from 2000 to 2008, presented a new 2400 cc turbo-diesel version that included a new transmission, new interior and ventilation system. The soul of the vehicle, however, remained the same: hard, pure and appreciated by army, police and fire departments around the world.

The last chapter of the Defender has not yet been written. After the Indian group Tata acquired Land Rover in 2008, new industrial projects developed and talk began of a completely redesigned model for 2013. This is something of a sacrilege to purists, as the Defender is conceptually true to 1948's Type 1 and still very structurally linked to the 90 and the 110 of the '80s.

Naturally, a legendary vehicle like this found a place on the big and small screens. There are coulless nature documentaries in which the car plays big part, but it has also had major roles in *The Itali Job* (1969); *The Passenger* (1975); *Tomb Raider* (200 which included the release of special commemor tive versions; *Bad Boys II* (2003); *Hotel Rwan* (2004); *The Da Vinci Code* (2006) and *Quantum of S lace* (2008). In addition, Land Rovers have appeare in the TV series *Dallas*, *MacGyver* and *The Simpson*

106 The Land Rover Defender owes its fame to its incredible versatility. It can be ordered with a single or double cab; a long wheelbase or a short one; and in pick-up, van, soft top or hard to configurations to meet any operational requirement.

106-107 The current generation of the Defender, unveiled in 2007, remains surprisingly faithful to the original style. But it is st. easily recognizable from previous models by the presence of a "hump" on the hood, which is needed to accommodate the 2.4 turbo diesel engine derived from Ford and also mounted on the Transit van.

From the Beetle's rib

To fully recount the history and evolution of the Porsche 911, you need to step back in time at least 30 years before the car's official 1963 debut at the Frankfurt Auto Show.

Ferdinand Porsche was a mechanical genius and one of the hottest car designers of the period between the two World Wars, so much so that, in the 1930s, Adolf Hitler commissioned him to design the Volkswagen Beetle.

In the meantime, Ferdinand's son Ferry, who worked with this father, had been nurturing an idea to build a sports car from the base of the Beetle and whose components, thanks to an agreement with Volkswagen, could now be used.

In 1948 the 356 model was born, bringing honor and glory to Porsche until developmental limits tied to its humble origins began to emerge, forcing the need for a more refined and versatile model.

110-111 The first Porsche, presented in 1948, was a 356 convertible with an engine capacity of only 1100 cc. The coupe version followed and led to the creation of a series of cars prepared for competition at the turn of the 1960s, as in the case of this 356 Carrera with a 1600 cc engine.

111 top Ferry Porsche, son of Ferdinand, pictured in 1958 between a 356 and a Beetle. Responsible for the development of Volkswagen, which was started by his father, Ferry used that experience and many of Volkswagen's mechanical parts to start building sports cars under his own name.

In the late '50s Ferry launched "Operation 911." Looking to maximize perfomance, he decided on a six-cylinder engine instead of the four-cylinder used for the 356, but he kept the cylinders mounted horizontally and embossed behind the rear wheels to lower the center of gravity for improved handling and to create enough space for the rear passengers.

The car was originally to be named 901, but Peugeot, which already had baptized its models using three-digit numbers with a zero in the middle, protested vigorously, and Ferry Porsche, after dozens of cars had already been built, decided to rename the car 911.

This fair play among rivals, however, did not stretch to sports. Porsche used the numerical abbreviations 904, 906 and 908 for some of its racing cars in the '60s and '70s, and Peugeot got its revenge in 2009 by winning the 24 Hours of Le Mans with a prototype it had baptized 908. Light and fast, the 911 immediately picked up the competitive racing legacy of the 356, becoming the benchmark on the track and, as long as its characteristics and regulations allowed, in rallies. This success even included wins in the large rally raids of the late '80s and victories in the Paris-Dakar competition in 1984 and 1985.

The first 911 had exceptional performance but also a wild, tameless character which endeared it to professional drivers. But it was cumbersome for regular drivers in dry weather and downright dangerous on wet surfaces. Some even tried to stabilize the car's reaction by loading the boot trunk with sandbags , while others tried this in the trunk to balance the weight of the engine.

Little by little, Porsche tried to correct these defects, lenthening the wheelbase in 1969 to make the car's nervy handling and reaction less abrupt, gradually changing the aerodynamic configuration with the appearance of a front spoiler in 1972 and varying the adjustment and layout of the supension.

Nevertheless, the original design and structure remained unchanged until 1997, despite the continued increase in displacement from 2000 to 3000 cc and in power from 130 to 400 hp. This care and refinement, however, greatly increased the 911's production costs, and that, combined with the lukewarm reaction received by newer models like the 924, 928 and 944, brought Porsche to the brink of failure around 1990.

To avoid collapse, it was necessary to modify certain concepts from the original project that were too expensive and, above all, to revolutionize the manufacturing process of the car using the expertise of engineers from Japan.

112-113 The 911 was born in 1963, when the 356 had already reached its developmental limits. Compared to its predecessor, it had a 6-cylinder engine instead of a 4-cylinder but kept the same boxer shape inherited from the Beetle. After the coupe, the Targa version was presented in 1966 (a 1986 model is shown here) and the convertible in 1983.

113 top The style of the first 911, designed by Ferry Porsche's son Ferdinand Alexander, also known as "Butz," has become a classic. It has remained almost unchanged until 1998, when the company revolutionized the car in the midst of a financial crisis.

The time machine

The result was the second generation 911 in 1997, which had a body inspired by the design of the original historical model and still had a rear six-cylinder engine. But the last remnant of the Beetle was abandoned: the cylinders were now cooled by water, not air. To increase sales, the supension was changed in order to obtain a more malleable and secure handling, while the dimensions (as well as the weight) underwent a sensible increase to improve liveability and comfort.

"The only flaw of the Porsche is Porsche drivers,"

it was once said, referring to the traditionalism of the most faithful clients, who did not take kindly to deviations from Ferry Porsche's original project. Indeed, the new 911 created some initial discontent among the car's most passionate supporters despite the improvement in performance. Gradually, however, these holdouts recognized the validity and effectiveness of the changes, and sales, helped by the company's continued sporting success, rose despite the notion that the car had become more comfortable and "docile." In short, Porsche's soul had remained intact.

The improved affordability of the new car led to an extraordinary sales boom and the company became the automobile world's version of the goose that laid golden eggs. Thanks to the introduction of successful models like the Boxster and Cayenne, Porsche's economic and financial power reached such heights that it even attempted a takeover of the giant Volkswagen in 2009.

Since evolution is in the Porsche genes, the 911 was renewed in 2005 and incorporated features of the first generation that were dear to nostalgists, such as round headlights and wider, more sinuous sides. This caused a further bump in sales, which was also driven also by an increase in power that has now passed the 500 hp threshold.

Nearly fifty years after its debut, the success of the 911 may best be summarized by the words of Ferdinand Porsche: "Being able to do something that will survive time, something that remains untouched by the eccentricity of individual eras, in short, something timeless: this is the biggest achievement."

It is no coincidence that the 911 has always been a fashionable item. It was the favorite car of maestro Herbert von Karajan and also movie star Steve Mc-

Queen, who was a big fan of auto racing and drivers. In the '70s there were few professional football players who did not have one in his garage, and even today it is still the car of choice for David Beckham, Arnold Schwarzenegger, Patrick Dempsey and Tom Cruise.

The car itself also continues to be something of a movie star, appearing not only in movies with an automotive theme such as *Le Mans* (1971) and *Cars* (2006) but also in comedies and action films like *Flashdance* (1983), *Against All Odds* (1984), *Bad Boys* (1995), *Nine Months* (1995) and *Mission Impossible* (2000) and many television series, including *Californication*, *Dallas*, *Special Squad Cobra 11*, *Smallville*, *Miami Vice* and *Melrose Place*.

The Porsche 911 is timeless, then, but also without boundaries.

116-117 The Turbo Cabriolet is one of the most fascinating current models. One feature that has contributed to the success of the 911 is its ability to combine high performance with versatility and reliability, which encourages daily use, something many of its sports car rivals cannot say.

117 top The turbo engine is one of the Porsche workhorses and it has been behind the best performing versions of the 911 since 1975. At that time, it could generate 260 hp but had a brutal, untamed temperament. These days the engine can exceed 500 hp but has become much more manageable.

118-119 The myth of the 911 has been continuously fed from racing, an area where the car has distinguished itself by winning almost everything possible. The GT3 version, which is lighter and more powerful than the standard model, serves as a base for cars designed for the track.

120-121 The Carrera name, introduced in 1955 to celebrate victory at the Carrera Panamericana in '53 and '54, was initially used to identify the sportiest Porsche, but from the mid '80s on it has come to characterize the vast majority of 911s.

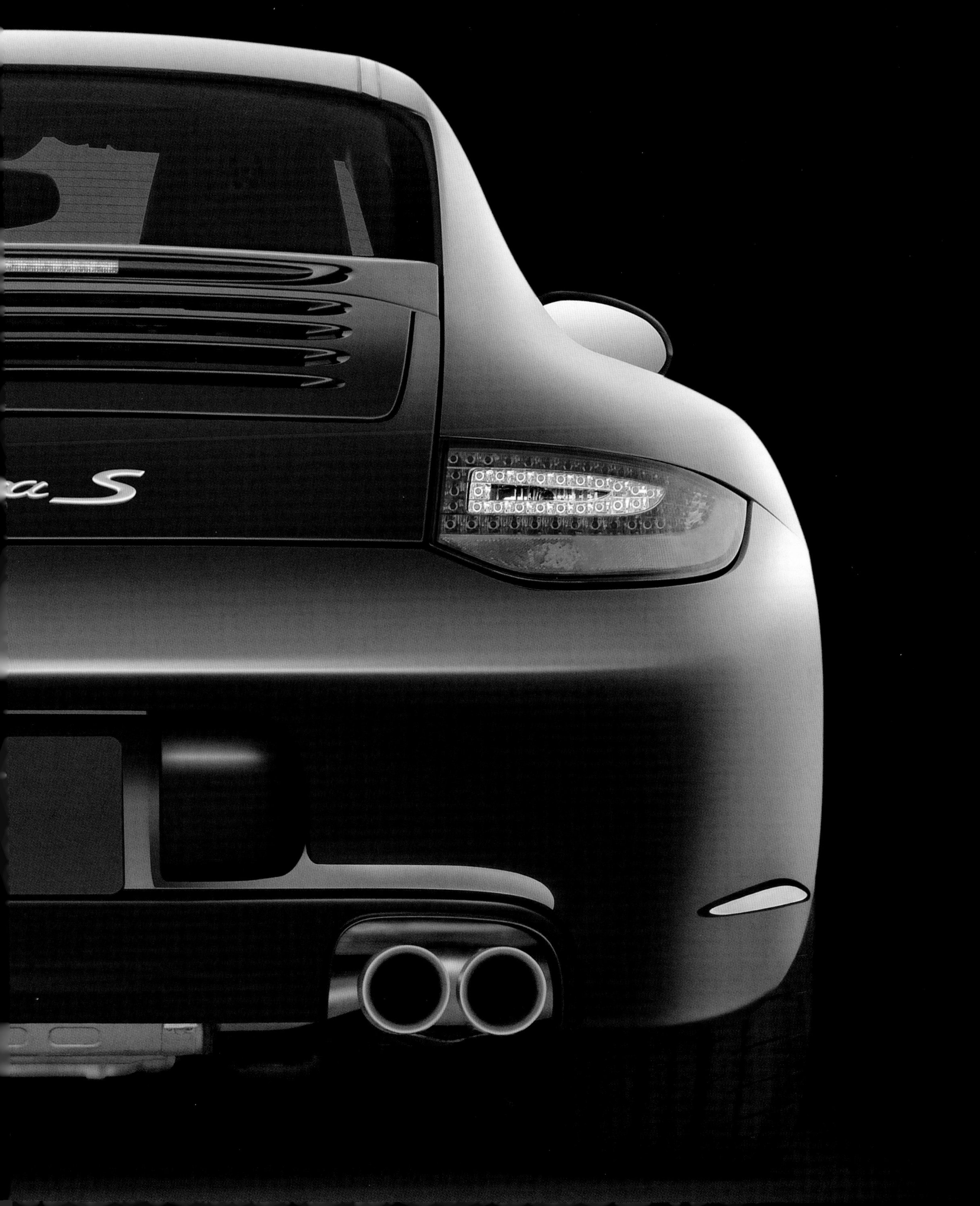

Citroën
2CV and C3

The farmer's car

Only those who go against the current become icons. One must be courageous to win the hearts and minds of people.

The Citroën 2CV has survived five decades and helped transform the automobile into a primary human need. Anticonformist, timeless, immortal: these are just some adjectives to describe a car born for the countryside that later conquered European cities. What were its weapons of seduction? Apparently very little. It wasn't potent, fast or very luxurious. The Citroën 2CV instead had bet on practicality and charm, which proved to be a winning combination.

The idea for the 2CV came to Pierre-Jules Boulanger, president of Citroën, in the middle of the 1930's. At that time, there were few cars on the road and many horse-drawn carriages. For farmers and ordinary people, traveling by motorized means was still too expensive and cumbersome.

The project TPV ("Très Petite Voiture," or "very small car") started in 1936. The task of designing the car was entrusted to Varese-born Flaminio Bertoni, the author of "Traction Avant" as well as the eventual creator of the DS. André Lefebvre, the brilliant inventor and driver who won the Rally of Monte Carlo in 1927, was brought in for the mechanics.

Boulanger's directions were clear and non-negotiable: the TPV had to be economical and simple to use but also capable of transporting four passengers plus 100 pounds (50 kg) at a speed of 35 mph (60 km/h) while consuming only 1 gallon (3 liters) of gas every 60 miles (100 km).

Boulanger himself verified that each of his provisions was met to the smallest detail.

For example, he sat in the car with a hat on his head to check the height of the space inside and even tested the softness of the suspension by crossing a plowed field with a basket of eggs on the seat to see that they wouldn't break.

After a few experimental prototypes that included motorcycle engines and simple canvas roofs, the final version was ready in 1939.

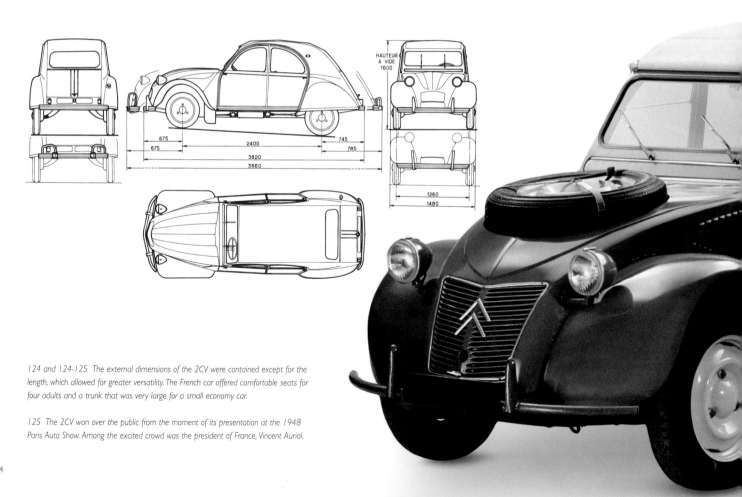

124 and 124-125 The external dimensions of the 2CV were contained except for the length, which allowed for greater versatility. The French car offered comfortable seats for four adults and a trunk that was very large for a small economy car.

125 The 2CV won over the public from the moment of its presentation at the 1948 Paris Auto Show. Among the excited crowd was the president of France, Vincent Auriol.

126 top With the "Deuce," functionality traveled hand in hand with fun. Some customers passionate about camping turned the trunk into a miniature kitchen and dining room complete with a folding table.

126 bottom A stamp from Gabon celebrating the 30th anniversary of the 2CV. The car has always had a close relationship with the postal service. In 1958 it became the first car ever depicted on a French stamp, and by the mid-'60s over 10,000 "postal van" models delivered mail to residents on either side of the Alps.

127 "The joy of living." So read one of many publicity posters. Carrying seven people (five children) in a small car without seat belts would now be foolish behavior, but this was all in a day's work for a motorist in the '50s.

REPUBLIQUE GABONAISE 200F

POSTES 1978

FORGET

Berline 2 cv. 1948

ANDRÉ CITROËN 1878-1935

The twin-cylinder engine was water cooled, equipped with a starting crank (even when it came with an electric starter, the 2CV always kept the hole in the nose to allow for any possible emergencies) and the body was made of aluminum alloy, except for the hood and fenders, which were made of sheet steel and canvas. The roof started from the windshield and ended at the rear plate.

There was only one light, both in the front and rear (which was in accordance with that era's traffic laws), and also no turn signals, so the driver had to use arm signals. This explains the presence of "flap-up" windows, which allowed the lower part of the window to pivot or tilt open, a feature that was retained even after the inclusion of turn signals.

However, when everything was ready to be presented at the Paris Auto Show, the Second World War began, and almost all of the 250 TPVs produced were destroyed to avoid having them fall into Nazi hands. Only five were saved, either buried, dismantled or hidden in barns. Meanwhile, work continued on the refinement of the car. The water-cooling system, which suffered in the cold, was abandoned in favor of a simple air and aluminum cooling system. However, since the cost of aluminum had taken off during the conflict, it was eventually replaced with steel, which was cheaper.

After many years of waiting, to the point that the press started to call the TPV "tourjours pas vue," or "still haven't seen," the 2CV (the number of the French horse tax necessary for the calculation of taxes) appeared at the Paris Auto Show on October 7, 1948.

The reception from journalists was cold, but for the public it was love at first sight. Sales of the car started on September 22, 1949, and already by 1950 the waiting list had grown to six years.

The reason for this success? The low price (it was roughly half the price of a Beetle), the reduced operating costs and the ability to adapt to just about any surface thanks to its wide excursion suspension, which was also the cause of its characteristic waddling gait. Furthermore, compared to the Volkswagen it had four doors instead of two and the front engine permitted a roomy trunk.

In addition to these features, there were also other interesting inventions. For example, the wiper was connected to the transmission so that the speed of the auto and that of the blade were proportional. Also, 1955 saw the introduction of an automatic centrifugal clutch which did not need to be employed with the motor running and a gear inserted.

128 The Citroën is now part of French popular culture, just like the Eiffel Tower and baguettes. In Alsace, between the towns of Schirmeck and Grandfontaine, a museum completely dedicated to its story was built.

129 In September 1974, the 2CV underwent its last cosmetic changes. The traditional rounded lights returned after a rectangular version was used briefly, and the grill and bumper were revised. They would remain virtually unchanged until the end of production in 1990.

Miraculously, the 2CV is able to accommodat

hat other cars would only refuse.

130-131 Thanks to the height afforded by the large canvas roof, the car effortlessly carried even the bulkiest of items. The roof was also easily disassembled to be cleaned and it attracted people of all ages with its retro design, which was something corporate advertising could not disregard.

The success of the 2CV dimmed slightly towards the start of the '60s with the arrival of the Renault 4, which had combined the concept of the "Deuce" (the nickname fans of the 2CV had given it) with a much more powerful engine and a hatchback.

The response from Citroën arrived in 1967 with the Dyane, which was similar to the 2CV but was more angular, livelier in its performance and more practical. Like its rival Renault, it too had a hatchback.

Citroën president Pierre Bercot wanted to re-place the "Deuce," but that was not how things un-folded. The career of the Dyane ended in 1984 after nearly 1.4 million cars were produced, while its older sister survived another six years, surpassing 5 million units sold, including a van version used commercially.

In its 42 years of existence the 2CV remained true to itself. The most important changes were in creases to the displacement (375, 425 and eventuall 602 cc) and the inclusion of front disc brakes in 1980.

Today it is still popular with collectors. The mos coveted version might be the Sahara twin engine (one front and one rear) with four-wheel drive tha was produced from 1958 to 1966.

Not to be forgotten is 1980's two-tone

Charleston, and also the rare 007 from 1981, created to commemorate its role in the James Bond movie *For Your Eyes Only*. Perhaps to sell off 2CVs that still had front drum brakes, 500 special editions were made. These were painted yellow with 007 written on the doors and small stickers imitating bullet holes along the sides.

small French car. It is in the films *American Graffiti* (1973) and *Apocalypse Now* (1979), and in the 1960s TV series *The Saint*. More recently, in 2001 it appeared in the Italian movie *The Revolution on Two Horses*.

Since July 27, 1990, when the last 2CV, a grey Charleston, left the Portuguese plant in Mangualde, Citroën designers have worked diligently to find a

132 You can't talk about the 2CV without mentioning French cinema. In the 1965 comedy blockbuster The Sucker, a 1958 2CV was destroyed in an accident involving actor Bourvil, who starred in the film with Louis de Funès.

133 The "Deuce" was used in The Soft Skin, a 1964 film directed by François Truffaut that was presented at Cannes.

Nostalgic curves

134 and 134-135 Initially Citroën designers hoped to reinterpret the sliding roof of the famous 2CV in a modern way by replacing it with a large glass area. The idea, however, was not followed through for the first C3 and eventually evolved into the very large windshield used for the current generation of the car.

Style Citroën Research*

The prototype CE Concept presented at the Paris Auto Show in 1998 whet the appetite of fans, but they had to wait until the 2001 exhibition in Frankfurt to see a market-ready model. In some respects the first C3 brought the 2CV to mind – it had an arched roof and similarly developed bodywork. But many other aspects were subject to the laws of aerodynamics. For example, the original prominent headlights were now gone. Despite having many elements in common with the Peugeot 206, such as the base mechanics and the rearview mirror, the C3 managed to distinguish itself with a playful style and great environmental awareness. Aside from gas and diesel options, the C3 was available with LPG or natural gas engines as well as with the start/stop system, which turned off the engine during stops.

In 2003 the C3 Pluriel, which also drew inspiration from the 2CV, made its debut. There may have only been two doors, but the sliding canvas roof and the revival of the Charleston in 2008 with a two-tone, black-purple version gave nostalgics reason to cheer.

The spirit of the original 2CV, however, has been difficult to recreate. The second generation C3, presented in 2009, further reduced the link to the past, especially when it came to the economical spirit that underlined the "Deuce."

List prices are now in line with rivals, and chic accessories like panoramic glass roofs and scents for the cockpit are available. The descendant, in short, does not go against the tide, so, unlike its "grandmother," it has not elevated from a successful model to become an icon.

PSA PEUGEOT CITROËN

Bentley Continental

A display of power

138 top The practical qualities of the R-Type sedan remained unchanged even in the first generation of the 1952 Continental coupe, which was built on the same platform. The performance of the car was improved in 1954 thanks to engine modifications.

138-139 Powerful engines, sleek and elegant design, chic and luxurious interiors: the first generation Continental was the most exclusive car of the '50s but, in keeping with Bentley tradition, did not need to flaunt this superiority.

Treating Bentley as a mere luxury brand can be limiting. It would be like judging a painting by its frame. In fact, many measure the English carmaker with the same yardstick as that of Rolls-Royce, and with good reason considering that between 1931 and 1998 the two companies were part of the same group and made many models together. But if Rolls has always represented the ultimate in stern, almost aloof, elegance, the Bentley has had more of an outgoing spirit since its inception. Not many know, for example, that the "real" James Bond (that of the original Ian Fleming books, not the film character) drove a Bentley, and even fewer know that the car with the winged "B" on its radiator has won six 24 Hours of Le Mans races:, in 1924, 1927–1930 and 2003.

To celebrate these great sporting achievements, many models past and present have been named after the straights and curves of the legendary French circuit: Arnage, Hunaudieres, Mulsanne. The one that inaugurated this tradition, the Continental, is also the car with the most fascinating story.

In 1952, the Continental name was used for the two-door version of the flagship "R," with an aluminum body instead of steel. Meanwhile, the car was already making a splash in other ways, topping the list of most expensive cars in the world with its list price of 7208 pounds. The 4600 cc engine, which would be 4900 cc starting in 1954, was the same as the sedan, but changes to the carburetor and the transmission's discharge and gear ratio improved performance. Sold mostly in England, 165 of the 208 produced were made for left-hand traffic.

The 1955 S1 Continental was similar to the Rolls-Royce Silver Cloud I. In fact, the engine was the same as the previous generation, but the car was far more successful, with 431 sold in all. With the 1959 S2, based on the second generation of the Silver Cloud, the old 6-cylinder engine gave way to a much better performing 6200 cc V8. The S3, produced from 1962 to 1965, differentiated itself with twin headlights, a sportier gear ratio and a larger interior space.

After more than two decades away from the scene, Bentley engineers resurrected the Continental name in 1984 for their new car. Linked with the Rolls-Royce Corniche convertible, the car entered into pop culture yore only a year after its launch with the video for the Elton John song "Nikita."

The real revolution, both technically and stylistically, came in 1991 with the Continental R coupe, the first Bentley since 1965 to not to have a "duplicate" Rolls. The R coupe was the fastest, most expensive and powerful car in the Bentley lineup. Pre-

sented at the 1990 Geneva Auto Show as a concept car, the official version made its debut the following year at the same exhibition. Many affluent customers rushed to acquire one, and the Sultan of Brunei, a known car lover, even bought one immediately at the show. The rest had to limit themselves to window shopping and dreaming.

The smoother lines represented a clean break with the past. The performance of the 6750 cc turbo engine, with 325 hp, a four-speed automatic transmission and a top speed of 138 mph (220

km/h), was excellent. Over time the car continued to evolve. The 1994 Continental S, produced for one year in a limited run of eighteen, mounted an intercooler to increase engine performance. The 1996 Continental T, in a 2+2 configuration, had a smaller frame to enhance handling, a chrome-finished interior instead of wood and an ignition button similar to that found in race cars.

The T line grew in 1999 with the introduction of the Mulliner, which had a stiffer suspension system, and the SC Sedanca, which came with a removable

A tank full of technology

140-141 The Continental GT was the first model of the "new" Bentley, an era that began with the acquisition of the English brand by the Volkswagen Group. The GT features a 6000 cc, 12-cylinder, 560 hp engine derived from those used in the Audi A8. Its maximum speed is nearly 200 mph (320 km/h).

142-143 The Flying Spur sedan was derived from the Continental GT coupe in 2005. The goal of ensuring a Bentley-like space for rear passengers was achieved by lengthening the wheelbase by 12 inches (32 cm) and the frame by 20 inches (51 cm). These changes, however, made the overall design a little less graceful.

roof that covered the front passengers. Only 73 SC Sedancas were produced, one of which is owned by former boxing champ Mike Tyson.

Bentley's addition to the Volkswagen line led to a decidedly noticeable change of direction. The Continental GT 2003, for example, was less exclusive than its ancestors, with many components shared with the Audi A8, but much more advanced in technology and performance. The modern styling, mighty 12-cylinder, 6000 cc turbo engine and permanent all-wheel drive brought immediate success. The four-door Flying Spur was released in 2005 and the GTC convertible came out the following year. The success of these models caused Bentley's annual production to rise from 1000 to 9200 cars produced between 2003 and 2006.

The following years saw the arrival of sportier and more exclusive versions. The 2007 Speed, which was more lightweight and powerful and capable of reaching 201 mph (320 km/h), was released in 2007, and in 2009 the Supersports, which has 620 hp and can run on either gas or ethanol, came out. That same year also saw the release of the GTZ, with bodywork by Zagato.

Volkswagen's involvement, considered scandalous by purists, actually reinforced the Bentley image by returning the line to its traditional sporting spirit. The increase in production volume was not a blow to its exclusivity but rather the only way to survive in an increasingly global market. Wealthy clients, after all, will always exist, and the only way to attract them is to be seen, not to hide in the shadows.

Chevrolet Corvette

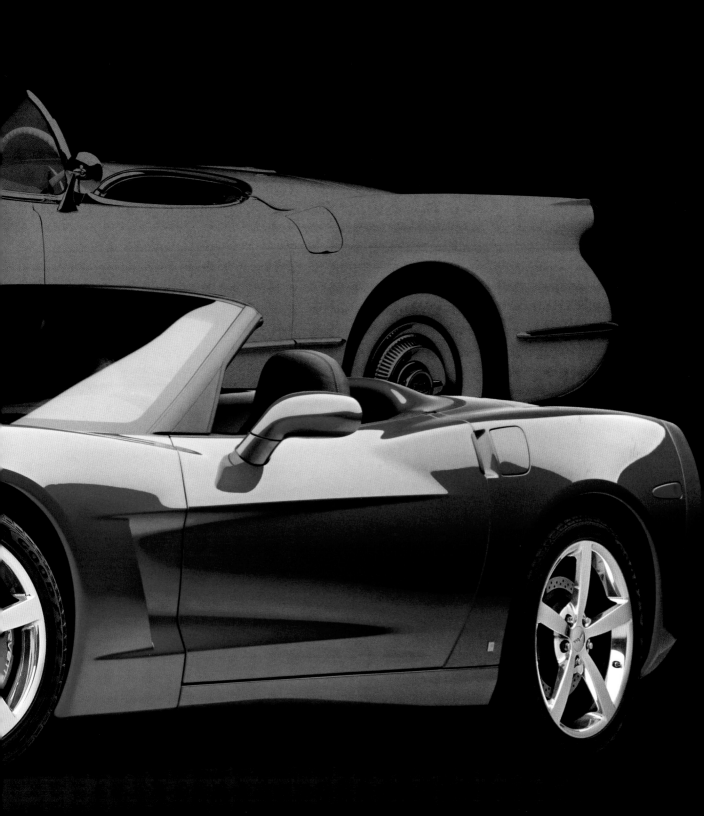

"It's not exotic. Exotic is producing 300 cars a [year?] and selling them at scandalous prices." These [wor]ds, spoken by Dave McLellan, Corvette's chief [eng]ineer in the 1980s, perfectly describe the phi[los]ophy at the heart of the most famous American [sup]ercar.

Potent but economical, the Corvette is capable [of] keeping pace with Ferrari, Lamborghini and [Por]sche despite being much simpler technically than [its] European counterparts.

In Europe the Corvette is little-known, mostly [be]cause Chevrolet has always favored the U.S. mar[ket], but in North America it is undeniably a cult phe[no]menon. In fact, it played a large role in the film [Cor]vette Summer (1973) and the TV series Route 66 [19]60 to 1964) and Stingray (1986 to 1987). It has al[so] appeared in many other movies, including Animal [Ho]use (1978), True Lies (1994), Apollo 13 (1995), Con [Air] (1997) and Austin Powers: The Spy Who Shagged [Me] (1999), as well as in music videos such as Ameri[ca]n Woman by Lenny Kravitz, Keeps Gettin' Better by [Ch]ristina Aguilera and What Comes Around by Justin [Ti]mberlake, not to mention TV series like CSI: Miami, [Mi]ami Vice, Baywatch and The A-Team.

The idea of the Corvette came about during the [Se]cond World War. At that time in America, cars [w]ere divided into two categories: simple and func[tio]nal or exclusive and luxurious.

Sports cars? They had yet to arrive. Back then, [A]mericans were satisfied with the elaborately heavy [h]ot-rods of the '30s, while some soldiers returning [fr]om the European front were bringing back, in their [h]earts and minds and sometimes literally, British ["s]piders" like the Jaguar and MG.

This gap in the market was filled in 1953 with the presentation of the Corvette C1. The designer of the first version, was Harley Earl, then in his 60s, who is still a legend in the U.S. Born in Hollywood, Earl began his career designing chariots for film studios. In 1938 he developed the first concept car in history, the Buick Y-job, and ten years later the iconic tailfins on the Cadillac, which would become a trend copied by nearly all major car makers worldwide. It was Earl who persuaded General Motors, which owns the Chevrolet brand, to build a "spider" that cost relatively little.

[14]6-147 In the first year of production the Corvette C1 [wa]s available only in white with a red interior and black roof. [Th]e styling was pleasantly sporty, but the 6-cylinder engine, [wh]ich only supplied 152 hp, was certainly not a highlight for [th]ose who loved to drive.

147 top The first Corvette left the assembly line in Flint, Michigan on June 30, 1953. For the first time in the history of a mass-produced car, the bodywork was made entirely of fiberglass.

The original Corvette had a light fiberglass body, an innovation which characterizes the car even today, but the engine was a "quiet" six-cylinder derived from commercial vehicles, and the disapointing two-speed automatic transmission was certainly not ideal for fun-loving drivers. Other issues were the water infiltration problems of the roof and the high price: despite predictions of a $2000 sticker price, the car ended up costing closer to $3500. The American public didn't like this increase, and while 300 cars were produced only 183 were actually purchased, with the rest given away to VIPs for promotional purposes. The following year the price dropped under $3000, which was still more expensive than the Jaguar and Cadillac. But this was misleading, as the transmission and handbrake, which were indispensable, had to be bought separately.

Sales remained far below expectations. In 1955 only 700 Corvettes were registered, while the rival Ford Thunderbird surpassed 16,000. The turning point came in 1957 with Belgian engineer Zora Arkus-Duntov, who decided to make the car more aggressive. He added to the list of options a powerful V8 engine and a manual transmission. Other innovations soon followed: an injection engine in 1957, ten years before it showed up in European cars; innovative dual mounted front headlights in 1958; and in 1961 four round rear lights, which are still a hallmark of the Corvette. That same year the engineers in Detroit built a four-seat prototype which was immediately rejected after the GM president got stuck in the rear pasenger seats.

The Corvette C2 of 1963 marked a revolution in the world of design, especially with the two-door Sting Ray version, which came with a split rear window.

The idea was shelved after only one year, however, because visibility was poor and the majority of customers chose the optional glass-only rear window. Worst of all, the car did not have a trunk, so bags had to be placed behind the front seats, and the rear suspension layout, which used leaf springs, was rudimentary and unrefined. By contrast, starting in 1965 four disc brakes would be standard on the car.

1968's C3 made improvements in the area of aerodynamics, while 1972 brought the introduction of an anti-theft alarm system after statistics had shown that one in every two Corvettes was stolen in its first year. Through these changes, the C3 became the most successful version of the car. In 1979, 53,807 were produced, and a year later a coach builder in California developed a four-door version. However, only five were ever assembled.

Conquering Europe

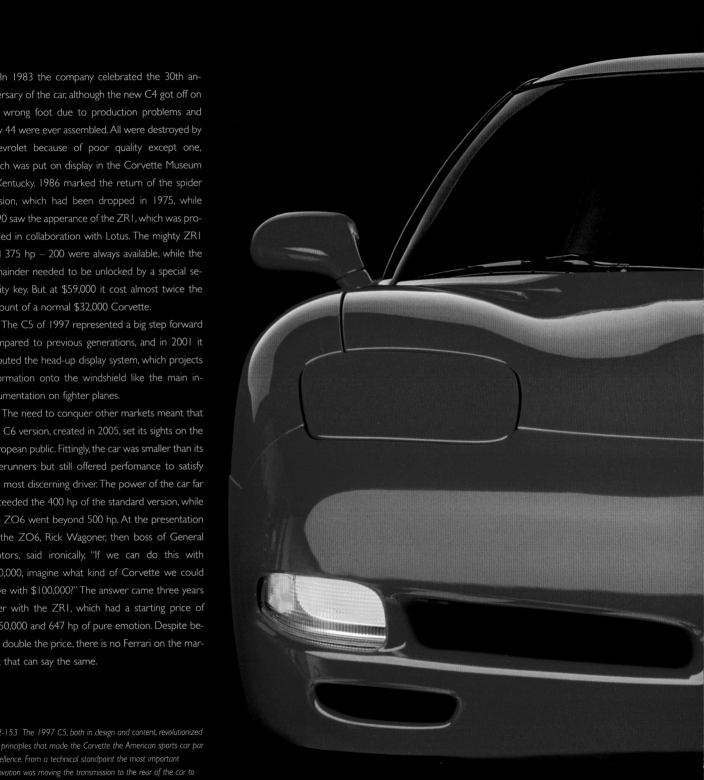

In 1983 the company celebrated the 30th anniversary of the car, although the new C4 got off on the wrong foot due to production problems and only 44 were ever assembled. All were destroyed by Chevrolet because of poor quality except one, which was put on display in the Corvette Museum in Kentucky. 1986 marked the return of the spider version, which had been dropped in 1975, while 1990 saw the apperance of the ZR1, which was produced in collaboration with Lotus. The mighty ZR1 had 375 hp – 200 were always available, while the remainder needed to be unlocked by a special security key. But at $59,000 it cost almost twice the amount of a normal $32,000 Corvette.

The C5 of 1997 represented a big step forward compared to previous generations, and in 2001 it debuted the head-up display system, which projects information onto the windshield like the main instrumentation on fighter planes.

The need to conquer other markets meant that the C6 version, created in 2005, set its sights on the European public. Fittingly, the car was smaller than its forerunners but still offered perfomance to satisfy the most discerning driver. The power of the car far exceeded the 400 hp of the standard version, while the ZO6 went beyond 500 hp. At the presentation of the ZO6, Rick Wagoner, then boss of General Motors, said ironically, "If we can do this with $60,000, imagine what kind of Corvette we could have with $100,000?" The answer came three years later with the ZR1, which had a starting price of $150,000 and 647 hp of pure emotion. Despite being double the price, there is no Ferrari on the market that can say the same.

152-153 The 1997 C5, both in design and content, revolutionized the principles that made the Corvette the American sports car par excellence. From a technical standpoint the most important innovation was moving the transmission to the rear of the car to

Mercedes
300SL and SLS

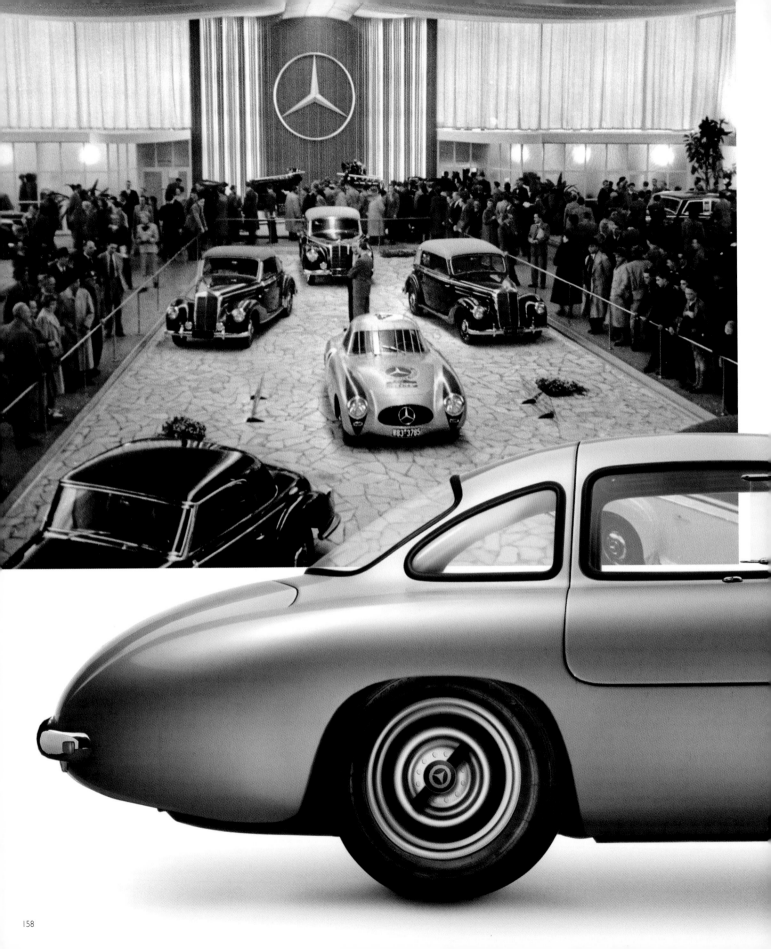

The happy seagull

In 1951, Daimler-Benz decided to return to competition with a sports car, believing that this would help the brand recover from the post-war crisis as quickly as possible. However, high costs and a scarcity of resources forced certain compromises. As a result, the 300 SL was created with existing elements that were not specifically designed for racing use.

SL was the abbreviation for "Sport Leicht," or "Sport Light," and 300 suggested a 3 liter displacement. In fact, the company used the 6-cylinder, 2996 cc engine mounted in the sedans of the time. Properly prepared, the engine in this new body could dispense 175 hp and 202 hp in the most advanced versions, a big improvement on the 115 hp of the sedans. Even the suspension and 4-speed transmission came from mass production. The aluminum body was designed specifically for the car, as was the lightweight tubular trellis frame that weighed only 110 pounds (50 kg), which created a trend among racing cars.

This structure, however, had a very high entry point which prevented the use of conventional doors. This forced the adoption of upwardly-hinged doors that allowed the driver to enter through part of the roof and whose opening evoked the flapping of a gull's wings. Hence the nickname "Gullwing," which has stayed with the 300 SL throughout time. This almost theatrical effect was quite remarkable for its period and it caused a great stir among sports car fans.

The development of the 300 SL was a very quick process. Conceived in June 1951, by November it was already on the track for testing, and by March 1952 it was presented to the press with a demonstration on the highway running from Stuttgart to Hailbronn. From there came a highly successful racing career that was abruptly interrupted in 1953 when the German carmaker decided to focus its resources on a return to Formula 1 the following year. But just when the story of the "Gullwing" seemed over, Max Hoffman, the American importer of European cars famous for his commercial intuition, pitched the company an idea for a road version of the car. Hoffman, in fact, went so far as to order 1000 SLs before the project was even approved.

158 top The SL seemed more like a spaceship than other Mercedes cars, despite the fact that many of its mechanical components came from standard production models. Its career, however, was brief. It lasted only a year because the German manufacturer chose to focus its resources on a return to Formula 1 racing in 1954.

158-159 The body was all aluminum and the tube frame weighed only 110 pounds (50 kg). The car debuted in 1952 with a second place finish at the Mille Miglia race and a win at Le Mans. Riding a wave of enthusiasm, Mercedes decided to enter the car at the difficult Carrera Panamericana in Mexico.

Mercedes smelled a deal, and on February 6, 1954, a prototype was presented at the New York Auto Show. The market version became available the following August at 29,000 marks, a price that was more than triple that of the 180 sedan of the same period. It should be remembered that at practically the same time, Hoffman took on a similar operation with BMW, convincing the Bavarian carmaker to develop the beautiful 507 for the U.S. market.

The road version of the "Gullwing" had a more elegant and modern front end, an elongated hood and air vents on the rear fenders. Even the tail had been redesigned to give greater impetus to the lateral view. The mechanics were much the same as its racing predecessor. However, it did come with a direct fuel injection engine that was designed for racing but never effectively made it on to a track. It was, in fact, the first car to have this technology as a standard feature. The weight had substantially increased since the body was no longer entirely aluminum. But thanks to the 215 hp, performance remained very high. The maximum speed was nearly 161 mph (260 km/h), which made the 300 SL the fastest production car in the world at that time.

The steering wheel could be dropped and tilted downwards to facilitate access to the driver's seat. The well-cared for dashboard was a thing of beauty, with a central aluminum strip between the upper and lower leather upholstery. Meanwhile, because the tail of the car was entirely occupied by the large gas tank and spare wheel, a luggage compartment was placed behind the two seats to compensate for the lack of a traditional trunk. Roughly 1400 units of the 300 SL coupe were built before being replaced by the roadster version to meet the demands of the American market.

160-161 During the 1952 Carrera Panamericana, the 300 SL driven by Karl Kling hit a vulture while traveling at over 120 mph (190 km/h). The impact shattered the windshield and injured navigator Hans Klenk. Despite this, the crew completed that portion of the race and ended up winning the hardest competition in Mexico.

Mercedes-Benz "300 SL"

III. Carrera Panamericana Me

1952

Leistung voraus

TYP 30

Den Gewinn aller Siege des Mercedes-Sterns
legen die Konstrukteure der Daimler-Benz AG. mit diesem Sportwagen
von souveräner Eleganz in die Hände ihrer Kunden.

162

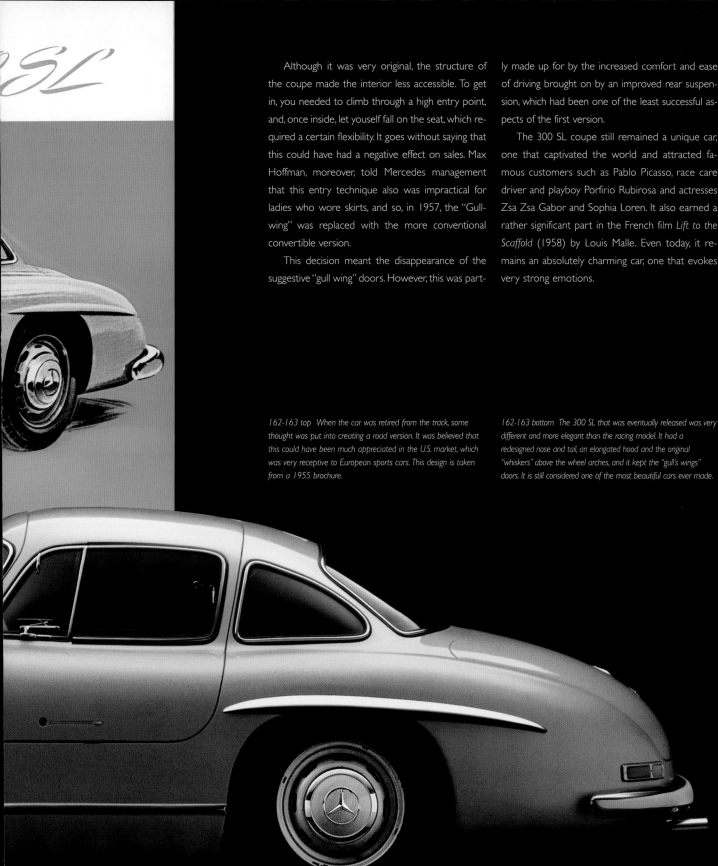

Although it was very original, the structure of the coupe made the interior less accessible. To get in, you needed to climb through a high entry point, and, once inside, let youself fall on the seat, which required a certain flexibility. It goes without saying that this could have had a negative effect on sales. Max Hoffman, moreover, told Mercedes management that this entry technique also was impractical for ladies who wore skirts, and so, in 1957, the "Gullwing" was replaced with the more conventional convertible version.

This decision meant the disappearance of the suggestive "gull wing" doors. However, this was part-ly made up for by the increased comfort and ease of driving brought on by an improved rear suspension, which had been one of the least successful aspects of the first version.

The 300 SL coupe still remained a unique car, one that captivated the world and attracted famous customers such as Pablo Picasso, race care driver and playboy Porfirio Rubirosa and actresses Zsa Zsa Gabor and Sophia Loren. It also earned a rather significant part in the French film *Lift to the Scaffold* (1958) by Louis Malle. Even today, it remains an absolutely charming car, one that evokes very strong emotions.

162-163 top When the car was retired from the track, some thought was put into creating a road version. It was believed that this could have been much appreciated in the U.S. market, which was very receptive to European sports cars. This design is taken from a 1955 brochure.

162-163 bottom The 300 SL that was eventually released was very different and more elegant than the racing model. It had a redesigned nose and tail, an elongated hood and the original "whiskers" above the wheel arches, and it kept the "gull's wings" doors. It is still considered one of the most beautiful cars ever made.

164-165 *The 300 SL was born as a racing car. The fascinating opening mechanism of the doors, described as the movement of a gull's wings, was not a gimmick but a necessity, as the chassis was so high at the sides that it made it impossible to use traditional doors. Meanwhile, the car boasted the first direct injection gasoline engine in history. This was developed for racing but never made it to the track, ending up on the 300 SL road version. Still, the racing spirit was alive and well, with the car's 215 hp giving it a top speed of 160 mph (250 km/h). This made it the fastest production car in the world.*

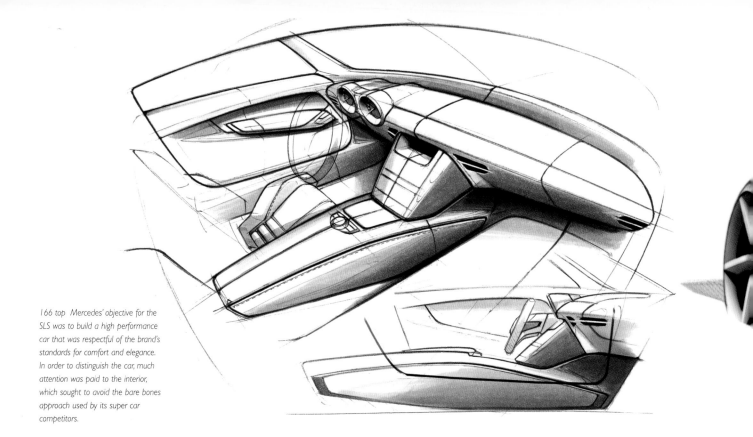

166 top *Mercedes' objective for the SLS was to build a high performance car that was respectful of the brand's standards for comfort and elegance. In order to distinguish the car, much attention was paid to the interior, which sought to avoid the bare bones approach used by its super car competitors.*

A festival of sharp edges

The spectacular "gull wing" doors remain in the hearts of Mercedes fans. The doors were used on the experimental 1969 prototype CIII, which was equipped with a Wankel rotary engine, but fans had to wait until the autumn of 2009 to see them on a production model again when the SLS AMG (an abbreviation of the Mercedes sports department) was presented at the Frankfurt Auto Show. The SLS AMG is a low, large and muscular coupe with a door opening system inspired by the first 300 SL but that lets passengers get in and out smoothly, despite the fact that the entry point is still only about 18 inches (45 cm) from the ground. In the design phase, the idea of using an electric door opening system was considered, but this would have added nearly 90 pounds (40 kg) to the weight so the project was abandoned.

The nose and front fenders reproduce the main stylistic elements of its ancestor, albeit with a more modern touch, but, unlike past models, the SLS has an all-aluminum chassis and body. The only exception is a few steel reinforcements for safety reasons. The engine is an 8-cylinder, 6-liter beast offering 571 hp, lightning-fast acceleration and a maximum speed of 200 mph (320 km/h).

The 7-speed transmission is mounted between the rear wheels to counterweight the presence of the large front engine. This gives the SLS the necessary road balance required for Mercedes to compete, on equal terms, with Porsche and Ferrari, brands that are far more familiar with this type of car. How does it plan to do that? By flying on the wings of a gull, obviously.

166-167 As shown in these sketches, the nose, tail and proportions generally tried to recapture the spirit of the first SL but with a modern spin. The design is entirely the work of the Mercedes design center, although many bodybuilders would have willingly worked on this project.

167 top Obviously, Mercedes could not part with the doors hinged on the roof, but it did allow a much larger entry opening than the cars of the '50s. The idea for an electric opening system was also considered, but this was abandoned due to the excessive weight it would have added.

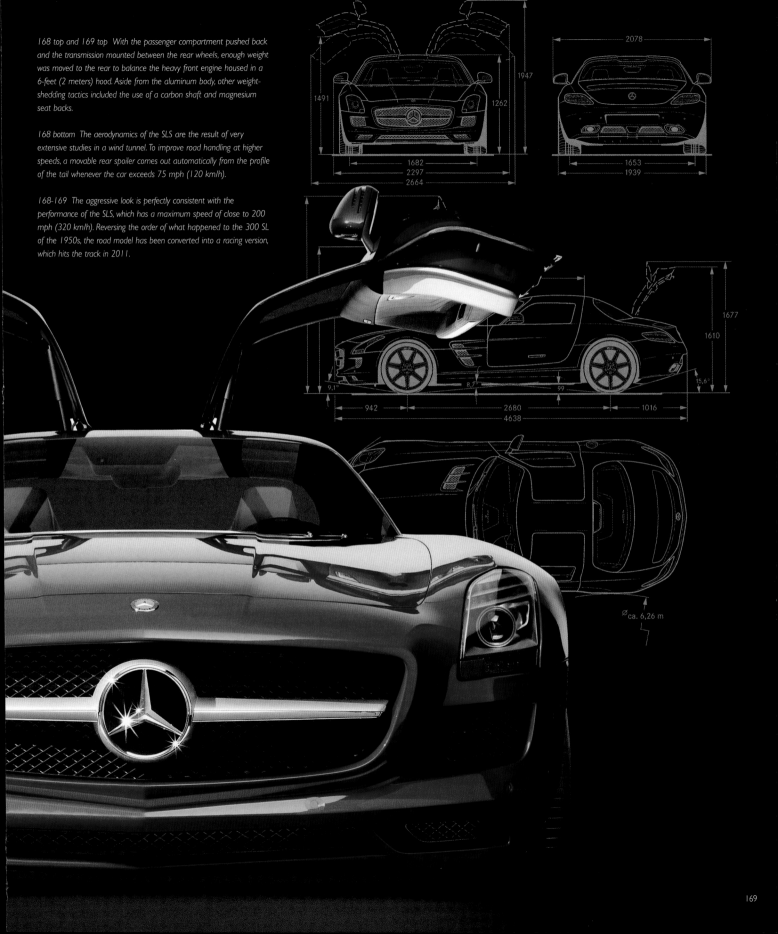

168 top and 169 top With the passenger compartment pushed back and the transmission mounted between the rear wheels, enough weight was moved to the rear to balance the heavy front engine housed in a 6-feet (2 meters) hood. Aside from the aluminum body, other weight-shedding tactics included the use of a carbon shaft and magnesium seat backs.

168 bottom The aerodynamics of the SLS are the result of very extensive studies in a wind tunnel. To improve road handling at higher speeds, a movable rear spoiler comes out automatically from the profile of the tail whenever the car exceeds 75 mph (120 km/h).

168-169 The aggressive look is perfectly consistent with the performance of the SLS, which has a maximum speed of close to 200 mph (320 km/h). Reversing the order of what happened to the 300 SL of the 1950s, the road model has been converted into a racing version, which hits the track in 2011.

170-171 AMG is the name of the Mercedes sports department, which for many years has prepared and maintained racing cars as well as create special high-performance versions of mass-produced models. For the SLS, AMG built a powerful 8-cylinder 571 hp engine.

Trabant 601 and nT

The economy car from another world

"Trabant" means "travel companion," and for nearly thirty years it was just that for a few million residents of East Germany. Its story begins in the 1950s in a divided Germany with the factories of Horch, a manufacturer of luxury cars founded by the father of Audi, August Horch. The factories were in the part of the country under Soviet control. Renamed AWZ ("Auto-Werke Zwickau," or "automobile factory of Zwickau"), the company started in 1954 by producing the P70, a funny little car with a twin-cylinder two-stroke engine, unsynchronized three-speed transmission and a body made out of Duroplast, a plastic material rein-

forced with cotton that is immune to rust, less expensive than steel, easy to shape and lightweight.

There is a downside to Duroplast – it is quite sensitive to temperature changes and over time tends to deteriorate and crack. Furthermore, even with a plastic base the car was not recyclable, despite what was seen in the 1998 Emir Kusturica film *Black Cat and White Cat*, where a large pig eats the entire body of a Trabant during the course of the movie.

In 1957 the company introduced the P70's successor, the P50, and dropped the AWZ brand name, becoming VEB Sachsenring (VEB the acronym for "Volkseigener Betrieb," or "the people's enterprise").

174-175 In profile the car reveals its extremely bare bones design, with a nose and tail almost the same shape as its straight sides. It seems like a toy car out of a comic and yet it was once the sole means of transport for millions of East Germans.

175 top Despite the fact that it was only 11 feet (3 meters) in length, the Trabant's interior was quite spacious. The diagram reveals the secret. The two-stroke engine was very compact and even the gas tank was placed under the hood to avoid wasting any passenger space.

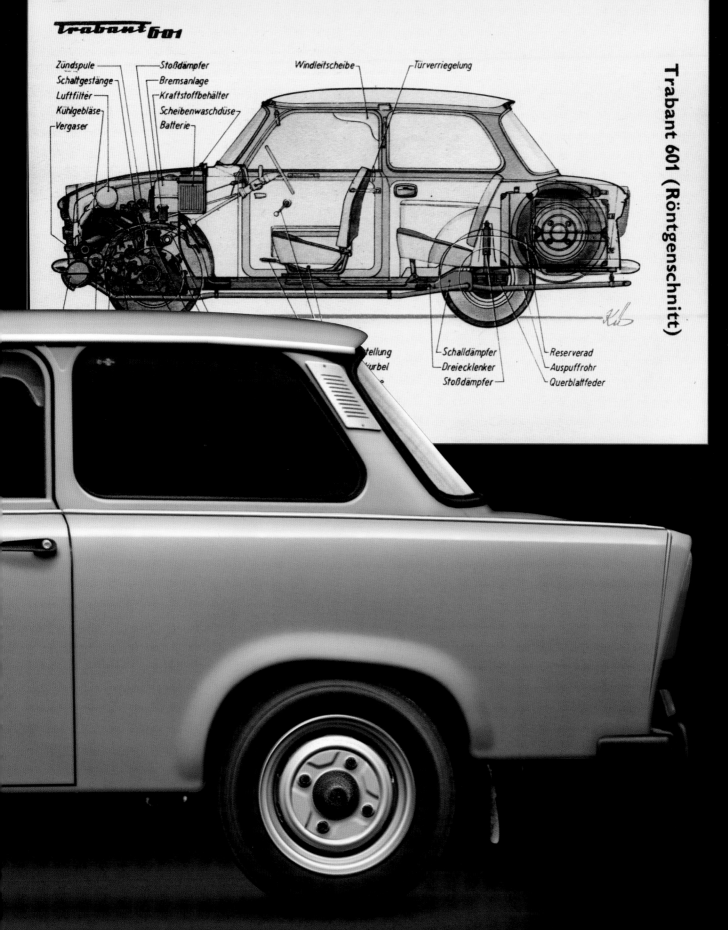

Trabant 601

Zündspule
Schaltgestänge
Luftfilter
Kühlgebläse
Vergaser

Stoßdämpfer
Bremsanlage
Kraftstoffbehälter
Scheibenwaschdüse
Batterie

Windleitscheibe

Türverriegelung

Trabant 601 (Röntgenschnitt)

...tellung
...urbel

Schalldämpfer
Dreiecklenker
Stoßdämpfer

Reserverad
Auspuffrohr
Querblattfeder

A contest was held to find a more creative name for the P50. Trabant was selected in honor of the first artificial satellite in history, Sputnik, which launched that year and literally means "travel companion" in Russian.

The P50 took the basics of the P70, but the 500 cc engine was given less power, with a reduction from 22 hp to 18 hp. Before the P60 arrived in 1960, 130,000 P50s with a slight increase in displacement were produced. However, the "real" Trabant, the one that we all associate with the Berlin Wall, had yet to arrive.

It came in 1964 with the 601 model, which remained unchanged until 1991, when it made its final exit from the scene. With 600 cc and 25 hp, the 601 was more nimble than the P50, although it did need 30 seconds to reach 60 mph (100 km/h) and it barely exceeded 70 mph (110 km/h). The structure and mechanics of the small sedan were mostly unchanged, with the same air cooling system and two-stroke, two-cylinder engine that caused smoke to spew from the car, but this time the vehicle had a four-speed transmission. If there was anything worth praising, it was the electronic ignition, which ran counter to the mechanically timed ignition systems based on platinum breaker points that the heavyweights of the Western automobile industry were using.

The electronic ignition had some advantages. For example, in 1997 a Trabant easily passed the so-called "FTAA test," the same stability test consisting of evading an obstacle at high speed that had only a few weeks earlier caused the newly created Mercedes Class A to roll over, a result that sparked an international scandal.

The 601 had a station wagon, the Kombi, and some convertible versions existed, though they were rare even if they were usually the result of "DIY" modifications. There was even one made for rallies – the 800 RS of 1986 – with an engine that had been increased to 800 cc and 65 hp.

The 601 was virtually the only means of private transport on four wheels that an East German could buy at reasonable prices. Not by chance, almost three million cars were produced. To obtain one, buyers were willing to accept waiting lists of several years. Rare second-hand Trabants were often more costly than new ones since they were immediately available.

In 1988, a year before the fall of the Berlin Wall, it was clear that something was coming. That year was significant for the "Trabi," as they had been affectionately dubbed by Germans, because it received a new "heart." The company transplanted the 45-hp four-cylinder engine from the Volkswagen Polo into the aging 601, which was built under license. The car, dubbed Trabant 1.1, also received a new suspension system to keep it on the ground with the new "insane" top speed of 83 mph (130 km/h) and a new grill, which was slightly retouched and closed on the right side.

The winds of change were knocking at the Brandenburg Gate and, in 1989, the Wall collapsed. Television around the world broadcast images of entire families riding in pastel Trabants and being feted by hundreds of citizens of the Federal Republic of Germany as they crossed into West Berlin, honking wildly.

This joyful moment, however, marked the end of the "Trabi," since East German inhabitants soon faced an almost infinite choice of Western models, both new and used, and subsequently dropped their old "travel companions." The factory was forced to close in 1991 after having assembled a little more than 39,000 Trabants with the new engine.

Recently, the Trabant has experienced something of a rebirth and prices have started to rise again. In addition to being exhibited at the GDR Museum in Berlin, which shows reconstructed scenes of life in the former East Germany, the cars can also be rented for a few euros.

A blue Trabant breaking through the Berlin Wall is one of the best-known graffiti images painted on the remains of the Wall itself, and its strong symbolic value has helped the car appear in over 200 films, including hits such as *Good Bye Lenin!* (2003) and *Confessions of a Dangerous Mind* (2002). The rock group U2 even made it the subject of the video for one of its most successful songs, 1992's "One," while also using eleven specially modified Trabants to illuminate the stage during its 21-month long ZooTV world tour.

176 It's the fall of 1989 and the end of the German Democratic Republic. A wave of Trabants cross the border in a bluish cloud caused by the emissions from two-stroke engines burning oil. These cars would soon be abandoned and forgotten by owners who for years had pampered them, often working on repairs themselves because auto service shops hardly existed.

177 The image of the Trabant breaking the concrete barrier to escape to the West is one of the most famous paintings on the remains of the Berlin Wall. The longest tract, measuring just under a mile (1.5 km), was dubbed the East Side Gallery and was recently restored.

A new
"green" life

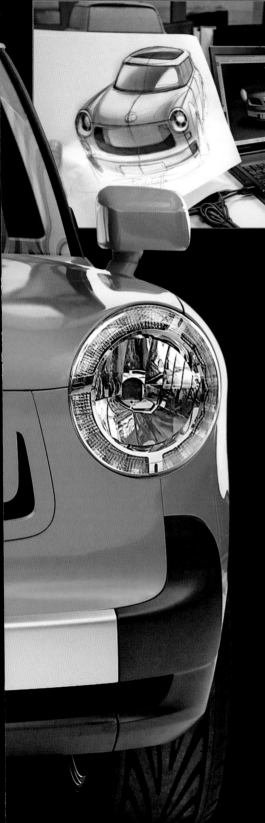

Although it was included in *Time* magazine's list of the fifty worst cars in history, a car like the Trabant, which symbolized both an era and a world view, was bound to inspire a new, modernized edition. And so at the 2007 Frankfurt Auto Show, the scale model of the Trabant nT concept appeared, looking indisputably like a Kombi for the 21st century.

Herpa, a well-known German carmaker, was the one to conceive the new idea, and in 2009, again in Frankfurt, the working version was unveiled. Designed by Nils Poschwatta, the new Trabant was produced by Indika, a company specializing in armored vehicles. If the old Trabi was nicknamed "forest killer" for the heavily polluted emissions of its two-stroke engine, the Herpa version is as green as can be. The engine is a 60 hp electric motor powered by lithium batteries. According to the manufacturer, this provides a range of 155 miles (250 km) and a top speed of 80 mph (130 km/h).

To see the car on the road, however, is going to require some patience, as a lack of funding has stalled production. You can buy a 1:43 scale model directly from Herpa for about $40 (30 euros), which is more than what some East Berliners would have asked for their original "Trabis" back in the fall of 1989.

178-179 The Trabant of the 21st century is linked directly to its predecessor and has tried to faithfully reproduce a style that, over the years, has become charming in the eyes of many.

179 top Designer Nils Poschwatta is working on a new edition of the "Trabi," almost fifty years after the birth of the original. To define its style, computer graphics have been used, as well as the classic clay models.

179 bottom The decision to replicate the station wagon version instead of the more famous sedan was caused by the need to accommodate the batteries. The tail lights incorporate the form of the original but with modern technology and LED lighting.

BMW 507 and Z8

Before the Second World War, BMW had been a respectable player in the spider/roadster field with the 328 Roadster. After the war, however, it found itself producing only sedans and without any real attractive products that could pull in new sales and customers. In America, especially, the demand for fast roadsters was exploding, as many returning American soldiers had been won over by light and aggressive European sports cars and many even imported the cars piece by piece. An enterprising BMW importer in New York named Max Hoffman was making a fortune and in 1954 he persuaded the German company to create a roadster for the American market.

Hoffman also introduced BMW to the young designer Albrecht Graf von Goertz, who soon got the job of designing the car. Within eighteen months, the first prototypes were ready. Two models of the 507 were presented in 1955 in the lobby of the luxurious Waldorf Astoria in New York. The design of the car earned enthusiastic reviews, leading some journalists to claim that BMW "had beaten the Italians." There was some truth to that since the car, despite being a purely German invention, had a provocative "Latin" design.

But the delivery of the first 507 didn't come until December 1956 because BMW at the time had prioritized the construction of the three-wheeled Isetta, a microscopically small vehicle that was something of a forerunner to the Smart car.

Under the 507 hood beat an 8-cylinder, 3.2 liter engine with only 148 hp, an amount that was only lightly augmented over the course of the model's life. The marketing brochure extolled the 136 mph (220 km/h) maximum speed, but few paid any attention to the note at the bottom of the page explaining how this result was reached by mounting a lowered windshield and a partial aerodynamic cover for the cabin. The 507 was therefore a fast car but not exactly a sports car, and its competitors, especially the Mercedes 300SL, had far superior performance.

This did not prevent the car from ending up in the hands of many prominent people. Elvis Presley, who served on a U.S. military base in Germany, was often seen driving a white 507, as was Alain Delon, Ursula Andress, the skier Toni Sailer, Rainieri of Monaco, the Aga Khan and the kings of Greece and Morocco.

182 and 182-183 The design of the 507 was originally drawn up by Albrecht Graf von Goertz, who later moved on to Porsche and then Toyota. The drawings and the resulting wooden model proposed a style that was not definitive, but they did demonstrate the presence of rear "wings," which were then all the rage in the United States but were eventually dropped in favor of a cleaner, leaner tail. The car, in fact, was intended for the American market, which was hungry for convertible sports cars after the Second World War.

183 top *Some American journalists claimed that BMW had actually beaten the Italians in style. It helped that this German pure breed had a provocative "Latin" design, even if the two bolts on the rear bumper of the prototype never came into production.*

The car wasn't a great success, mainly because of a very high price of almost 30,000 marks, which comes out to more than $20,700 (15,000 euros) at today's rate. In all, 521 cars were produced, plus three complete chassis designed for special projects, and only 39 of these hit the U.S. market for which they had originally been built. Consequently, production ceased in 1960.

Strangely, the 507 failed to tickle the imagination of filmmakers, despite its acknowledged beauty. Its only notable appearance on the big screen is a chase scene in *Fantômas* (1964), a French film in which, curiously, all the cars have a plate number ending with 75.

184 While stationed at an American Army base in Germany, the King of Rock 'N Roll, Elvis Presley, buys a 507 from a BMW dealer in Frankfurt. Handing him the keys is 1956 Hesse beauty queen Ursula Siebert.

184-185 The official name of the 507 car, "Touring Sport," can be seen on this promotional poster from 1957. If the design was very sleek and aggressive, the performance was not up to its image and prevented the car from really competing with its Italian rivals and also its compatriot, the Mercedes 300 SL. Still, the 507 never lost its charm, even with a hardtop in place of the fabric roof. This hardtop option, built entirely by hand, was only ordered by a few owners

186-187 Because of its high price, less than 520 units were sold and only 39 ever made it to the American market for which it was designed. Production was suspended in 1960.

BMW 507

Touring Sport

Tons of power (to avoid past mistakes)

History repeated itself in the early '90s with BMW again feeling the need to have a prestigious sports car that could give the brand some luster. In 1994, the Dane Henrik Fisker, who later moved to Aston Martin, presented his first sketches to the company. At the 1997 Tokyo Auto Show, the Z07 prototype made its debut, its name visually recalling the 507.

The car was obviously a tribute to its forerunner from the '50s, recalling the general stylistic approach with its long front end and very short tail. Furthermore, the hood was developed horizontally, with side vents located behind the front wheels. Much like in the past, audience reaction was very positive. In 2000, production of the car, dubbed the Z8, began, with the

architecture of the 507's V8 engine taken as well.

This last feature, much like all the rest of the mechanics, came from the M5 sedan, and its 400 hp propelled the Z8 from 0 to 60 mph (100 km/h) in 4.7 seconds. This speed was electronically limited to 155 mph (250 km/h) since BMW would not repeat the mistake of using an undersized and underpowered engine.

For its launch, the company used the same marketing road traveled by the Z3 in 1995. The Z8 was James Bond's car in the film *The World Can Wait* (1999), with one literally cut in half as part of the story.

The Z8 also had a very high price, one that put it in direct competition with heavyweights like Fer-

rari and Lamborghini. Furthermore, the car was not customizable, as it came fully equipped. There were no options and you could only choose the color of the body and interior. Despite this, between 2000 and 2003 there were 5703 produced, with 3160 staying in Europe and 2543 ending up in the United States. This came close to the original company estimates of moving 1500 a year.

The latest Z8 came off the production line in September 2003, just weeks after production ceased on its "organ donor," the M5.

188-189 Unlike its predecessor, the Z8 had a hardtop in mass production. The only option the car provided was a choice of interior and exterior colors. The aesthetic result, however, was questionable, so much so that it's rare today to see a hardtop model on the road.

189 top British actor Pierce Brosnan, one of the many actors to portray James Bond, poses next to the Z8 that starred in The World Is Not Enough. In the film the reinforced car had two retractable missile launchers on each side and could be guided by a remote control in the ignition key.

190 top The entire interior of the Z8 followed a deliberately retro style, starting with the thin metal steering wheel spokes and the instrumentation, which was positioned at the center of the dashboard by chief designer Chris Bangle, who wanted "to make it so that the driver could concentrate exclusively on the road and be one with the car."

90-191 The evolution of the Z8 from the 507 is especially evident in the front-end view. Not by chance, the prototype that appeared at the 1997 Tokyo Auto Show was named Z07, in a visual play on words that reclaimed the spirit and name of its ancestor from the '50s.

Ford Thunderbird

A sports car, so to speak

The Thunderbird is a mythical creature revered by some Native Americans. A bearer of storms, the movement of its wings is said to thicken the clouds while its eyes give birth to thunder and create the bright serpentine flashes of lightning that the bird carries and drops to the earth.

A name that aggressive seems poorly suited to a car that became famous for making luxury affordable. The name came from an internal competition for Ford employees, in which 5000 different ideas flooded in, including El Tigre, Apache and Thunderbolt. The winning entry came from designer Alden "Gib" Giberson. Initially the prize was a $250 designer suit, but Giberson settled for a $95 suit and a pair of trousers from Saks Fifth Avenue.

With the Thunderbird, Ford launched the concept of the personal luxury car – a high performance vehicle that was more compact and less expensive than the company's rivals. In fact, the car was too heavy to be considered a genuine sports car, but when properly equipped it was able to win several championships, including NASCAR. Its greatest success, however, came with the general public, as 4.4 million Thunderbirds were produced in a 45-year career.

The car's appeal was so wide that it was just as easy to see it parked in front of an exclusive club as it was to find it outside a supermarket. It was the graduation present many young Americans dreamed of but also a car loved by older women.

In short, the passion for the Thunderbird had reached nearly everyone.

The initial idea was the same as the Chevrolet Corvette – an American sports car capable of competing with European rivals. After several prototypes, the production model was adopted in September 1954 with a focus on interior comfort, despite the fact that the coupe and convertible versions only had two seats.

The technology on board was avant-garde. Among the available options was a Volumatic radio that raised the volume with the number of engine revolutions. Sales soon boomed, with 16,155 sold in 1955 compared to only 700 Corvettes, but the company was not yet completely satisfied.

194 top The first Thunderbird was not only the dream car of adults but also children. The toy version had working headlights, was powered by a battery and could reach 6 mph (10 km/h).

194-195 Perfectly in line with American tradition, the first Thunderbird initially only came with large 8-cylinder engines. Power ranged from 193 to 223 hp and the transmission, always a three-speed, could be manual or automatic.

For the second generation in 1958, the car was redesigned so that four passengers could be accommodated. The Thunderbird thus became wider, with a longer wheelbase and a weight increase of 880 pounds (400 kg). Thunderbird sales continued to grow, up to 93,000 in 1960.

The 1961 model, which had a shape that resembled a bullet, is one of the most beloved by fans. Robert McNamara, president of Ford and eventual U.S. Secretary of Defense, got fifty Thunderbirds to accompany President John F. Kennedy on the day of his inauguration. It was an incredible publicity stunt.

A central rearview mirror was used for the first time, and among the technological goodies was the ability to move the steering wheel 18 inches (45 cm) to the right to facilitate getting in and out of the car. Among the list of accessories was air conditioning and electric windows. While gadgets abounded, some were useless, such as the turn signal that lit in sequence from the inside to the outside for the entire width of the light. Other important elements were still missing, like front disc brakes, which were only introduced in 1965.

The real breakthrough came the following year. The fifth generation of the Thunderbird underwent numerous internal changes to avoid overlap with the more powerful and economical Mustang, which had been created three years before. Dimensions grew, the quality of the interior was improved and the convertible version disappeared to make room for a four-door, whose back doors were rear-hinged (this version, however, was not very successful). The overall style was inspired by fighter planes. Among the options was a system that automatically closed the doors once you exceeded 8 mph (13 km/h).

In 1971 the luxury goods store Neiman Marcus launched a rather original promotion aimed at couples – two specially designed "his and hers" Thunderbirds equipped with an electric razor, make-up mirror and tape recorders for $25,000.

The car's size continued to rise and swell, with the sixth edition in 1972 reaching its maximum length of 214 inches (540 cm), an increase of close to 120 inches (300 cm), and a weight of more than two tons (1800 kg) if you opted for the powerful 8-cylinder, 7.5 liter engine. The American car information source Edmunds wrote that this Thunder-bird had "doors about the size of a county in Kansas and a hood so long it was rated a par five by the PGA." The car consumed gas like an airplane and under certain conditions could only manage 8 miles (13 km) per gallon. When the oil crisis began, sales dropped sharply, from 87,000 in 1973 to 43,000 in 1975.

Recovery came with the 1977 version, which was just under 10 inches (25 cm) shorter, nearly 400 pounds (180 kg) lighter and with reduced total displacements of 4.9, 5.8 and 6.6 liters, although the engines were still 8 cylinders. This was the most popular Thunderbird of all time and there were more than 300,000 registered in ensuing years. However, the public soon demanded more compact sizes and efficient fuel consumption.

Suggestive but not well loved

In 1980 a 6-cylinder engine debuted, but the design did not attract people and the car was made more aerodynamic and sporty looking in 1983. A five-speed manual transmission was introduced, which joined the automatic and supercharged four-cylinder engine versions.

For the tenth generation in 1989, Ford tried to increase the driving pleasure by using a four-wheel

198-199 The Thunderbird of the 2000s, created to attract the nostalgic crowd, did not have a successful career. From 31,121 units produced in the first year of production in 2002 it fell gradually to 9220 in 2005. The total number of units produced was lower than the worst year of the previous generation.

independent suspension (a rarity in the U.S. for that category of car) and a slightly longer wheelbase, but the dwindling interest for four-door coupes forced Ford to stop production in 1997.

The luxurious Thunderbird had already won over audiences on the big and small screens. Aside from the convertible that famously took flight at the Grand Canyon in *Thelma and Louise* (1991), it also played a big role in *La Dolce Vita* (1960), *The Raven* (1994) and in the 1986 music video for Madonna's "True Blue."

But the career of the T-Bird, as it is often called, had not yet ended. Following the new retro trend in car design, which had already brought the Volkswagen New Beetle and the new MINI, Ford tried to resurrect its legend in 2002 with a reissue.

It was a real return to the origins, at least in look: a two-seater, '50s style roadster that combined a prestigious platform (shared with the Jaguar S-Type and XF) with a 3.9 liter V8 engine. Sales, however, were poor, despite the car being featured in the James Bond film *Die Another Day* (2002). Ford decided to end production of the Thunderbird in 2005 after three extra years of life that only managed to remind fans of a past that is unlikely to return.

Fiat 600 Multipla
and Multipla

Brilliant but
often laughed at

Italians do not like half measures, even in the automotive field. They are, after all, known for small cars and supercars and not so much for those in between. The Fiat 600 Multipla of 1956 is the most representative of what an engineer in the "Beautiful Country" can design with a very compact chassis.

Built in 1955 on the platform of the 600 – the car that began the motorization of Italy, a process completed by the 500 – the Multipla could carry six people despite being just over three feet in length, which is only thirty inches longer than a Mini. To do so, Dante Giacosa, the legendary Fiat designer behind the 500, 126, 127, 128 and the Autobianchi A112, advanced the driver and front passenger's seat up over the front wheels, which required the installation of the 1100 sedan's more robust suspension, to obtain space for two rear seats.

This was an innovative solution, but it certainly was not ideal for security and comfort. In order to not be too bulky, the seats were little more than upholstered chairs and whoever sat up front had his or her head practically against the windshield while the spare tire, jack and tool bag were also in front of their legs. The driver, meanwhile, had to deal with a nearly vertical steering column sandwiched between the clutch and the brakes. The Italian magazine *Quattroruote* promptly published a guide on how to sit in a Multipla.

The 600 Multipla was almost universally panned. However, since it was devoted to the cult of practicality, it found an audience. With its vertical front end and elongated tail without a hatchback, since the engine was in the rear, the car seemed as if it was always travelling in reverse. Road-holding and braking were average, and the performance of the 633 cc, 21.5 hp engine (raised to 29 hp in 1960) was very modest, especially at full load. The rear seats, however, could be lowered to form a flat, large loading area, an invaluable option for those who used the car as a business tool.

Its funny but fun looks fueled some brilliant film appearances, such as in the comedy *Buona Sera, Mrs. Campbell* (1968) and a chase scene in the hilarious Dino Risi movie *Operation San Gennaro* (1966).

From 1956 to 1965 the car was bought by 243,000 people, but it was derided by almost everyone else. In fact, in Italy it was mostly driven by taxi drivers (whose green and black Multiplas were once a familiar site on the streets of Rome and Milan), nuns and artisans. Outside national boundaries it remained virtually unknown.

202 top and 202-203 The dimensions of the 600 Multipla were very compact, with a length of just under 10 feet (3 meters). Despite this, the car could carry six people in three rows of seats and, if the rear bench was reversed, offered a load area of 19 square feet (6 square meters).

202 bottom One wonders what spectators at the 1956 Turin Auto Show thought when on April 24 they first saw this car with such a strange styling on display. Today it is still surprising to see how much space the interior had.

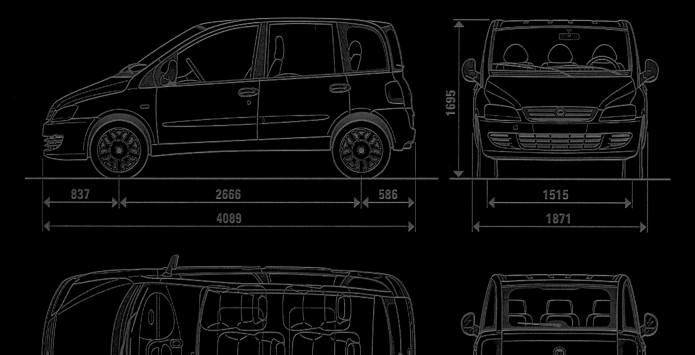

837   2666   586

4089

1695

1515

1871

1520

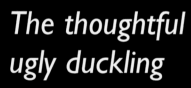

The thoughtful
ugly duckling

204 top The 1998 Multipla, although very different from its
ancestor, kept the same philosophy. To call its style bizarre would
be an understatement. The proportions were unusual, with six seats
in two rows of three and small external dimensions. In fact, it was
less than 14 feet (4 meters) long.

204-205 The most original part of the '90s era Multipla was
undoubtedly the "doughnut" placed under the windshield, where
the beams were placed apart from the main headlights. The idea
was that this innovation would be adopted by every Fiat model,
if it was well liked.

205 The ability to carry six people in two rows of three seats was
due to the considerable width of the body. Unfortunately, the central
front passenger could not be protected by a dedicated airbag.

Fittingly, Fiat made no further experiments until 1998. That year's Multiplia took advantage of the Brava compact sedan's platform but was 157 inches (400 cm) shorter in length. Nevertheless, the interior space was plentiful and there were still six seats, arranged in two rows of three. The design by Roberto Giolito, who also designed the new 500 in 2007, was very particular. Leaping out at you were the vertical sides, the disproportionately large glass surfaces and the "step" at the base of the windshield in which two additional headlights resembling tadpole eyes were included. The interior was no less interesting, especially with regard to the elaborate and futuristic dashboard.

At its debut, there were two engines available – a 1600 cc gasoline engine and a 1900 cc diesel engine – which performed well and were suspported by road holding and drivability superior to the best minivans on the market at that time.

In addition to being practical and innovative, the Multipla was also environmentally friendly. It was, in fact, one of the first cars to be sold with a dual fuel system (gas/LPG or gas/methane), partly because of the unique structure of the platform, which produced a sort of double bottom under the driver's

side, allowing the cylinders to be positioned with few modifications or effects on passenger and cargo space. The Multipla was also designed with a possible hybrid version in mind that would have an internal combustion engine with an electric motor. Some prototypes of these were actually made in 2000 in collaboration with the city of Naples. However, these were not followed up.

Criticism poured in on the new design, with *Time* magazine including the Multipla on a list of the fifty ugliest cars of all time. Cheekily, the Turin carmaker responded with the slogan "You are beautiful." Either way, the car was exhibited in 1999 at New York's Museum of Modern Art and

it appeared in the British science fiction film *Children of Men* (2006), which was set in a post-apocalyptic 2027.

That it was far from the ideal of classical beauty was widely accepted, but unlike its predecessor it met with great success, so much so that requests for the car went beyond Fiat's expectations. The people who bought did it to be proudly alternative, while others covered their eyes before getting in the car, even if they had to appreciate the car's genius and versatility, which was shown in 2009 when the Italian Financial Police stopped a Multipla that was illegally carrying 1700 exotic animals.

After undergoing the EuroNCAP crash test in 2001, the Multipla obtained an unsatisfactory rating in collision protection of both passengers and pedestrians in the event of a front-end crash. This required a redesign, which ultimately meant a "normalization" of style, one that could attract even those who had previously snubbed the Multipla.

The 2004 restyling proposed a more traditional, solid front end, which recalled that of other Fiat models. One of its most characteristic elements, the additional "tadpole" headlights, were dropped. Also, the external length was increased by nearly 4 inches (10 cm), thus alleviating the compact feeling that characterized the first series.

All of these changes, however, ended up just making the Multipla more anonymous and sales fell, leading the car to the end of its career. Italians have always loved exaggeration, after all, sometimes even when it runs counter to the common sense of beauty and the norm.

206 top If the square shape of the body gave rise to many aesthetic concerns, it also allowed a lot of space for luggage. By reclining the rear seats, the space available for loading rose above 70 cubic feet.

206-207 The decision in 2004 to replace the headlights mounted at the base of the windshield with a more traditional placement in the front end made the car much less unique. Maybe the marketing department thought that a less original front end would increase the number of customers. They were wrong.

207 top The latest cosmetic changes led to an increase of 4 inches (10 cm) in body length, which jeopardized the car's proverbial compactness. In 2010 the gas engine disappeared as well and the Multipla now is available only in methane and diesel engine varieties.

Ferrari California

The dream car of the jet set

The 250 California, built at the turn of the 1960s, was the Ferrari which, more than others, combined the spirit and soul of driving pleasure into one single car. It was one of the most fascinating roadsters in the world, a status -symbol that was also suitable for track competitions, at ease on a circuit or parked in front of the Casino of Monte Carlo. A symbol of wealth for those who had the means, the California was the essence of dream car for everyone else.

Brigitte Bardot and her former husband, director Roger Vadim, owned two, while writer Françoise Sagan, author of *Bonjour Tristesse*, drove his on the road as if gunning for a pole position. U.S. actor James Coburn, star of *The Magnificent Seven*, *The Great Escape* and *Pat Garrett & Billy the Kid*, owned a black California which in 2008 sold at auction for more than $7 million (5 million euros). Simply put, the Ferrari California hasn't needed to appear in many movies because it is itself a part of Hollywood.

The 250 GT Spyder California (the official name of the 1957 car) helped write the history of Maranello, even if indirectly. When Ferrari's German driver Wolfgang von Trips was killed at Monza in 1961, his parents decided to use a California for the last journey of the coffin.

The car took form when two Ferrari importers in the U.S. – Luigi Chinetti and John von Neumann – sent a proposal to Maranello for a roadster based on the legendary 1954 coupe 250 GT. Pininfarina occupied himself with the styling while Scaglietti worked on the construction of the body. Together, they were a winning team.

210-211 *Distinguishing a model with a long wheelbase from one with a short wheelbase is not easy. One obvious difference, besides the distance between the front and rear wheels, is the air intake on the hood. It protrudes on a long wheelbase and is partially integrated into the body on a short wheelbase, as seen in this car, which is also equipped with a removable hard top.*

Only 45 of the first version, dubbed LWB, or "Long Wheelbase," were made. It had careening headlights, a steel tube chassis and aluminum hood, doors and trunk hatch. The engine, the same as the 250 Tour de France, was a 3000 cc V12 with 240 hp that even produced good results on the track, as it finished fifth overall at the 24 Hours of Le Mans in 1959.

Performance was first on the list of priorities, with elegance and comfort not considered important. The only "chic" accessory, in fact, was a heater.

In 1960 the SWB (Short Wheelbase), at 95 inches (240 cm) instead of 102 (260 cm), got its turn and 55 were produced in the next three years. The distance between the front and rear wheels was reduced. Four disc brakes, a first for Ferrari, and 40 more hp, up to 280 hp total, increased the sheer pleasure of driving. Meanwhile, the door handles were recessed instead of protruding, the side vents for hot air had three slits instead of four and the last units assembled had a wider track.

212-213 Some units produced in 1958 had headlights that did not have transparent casings. The choice to adopt bulky auxiliary headlights that were about the same size as the grill depended exclusively on the customer's desire.

The well-bred "prancing horse"

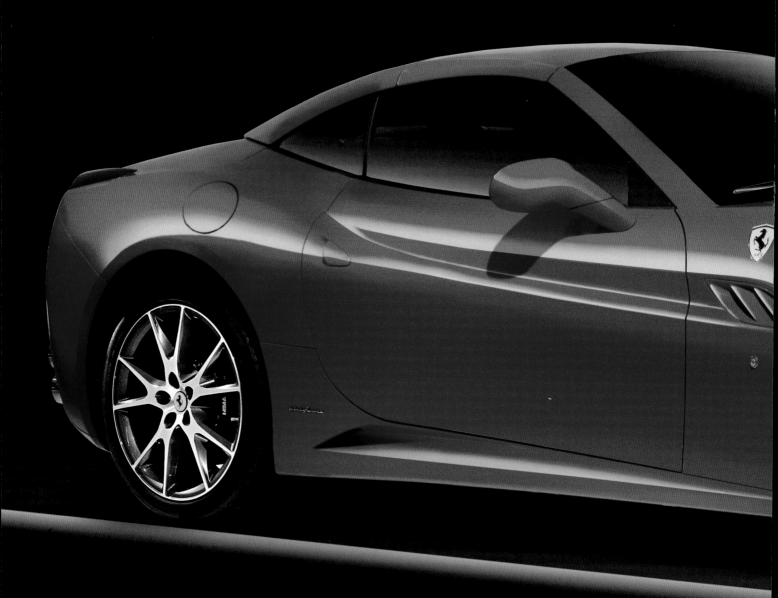

214-215 *The new California incorporates many stylistic elements of its predecessor, such as the side air vents, the air intake on the hood and the shape of the headlights, although these have been given a modern twist. The metal roof panel seems to be in conflict with tradition, but it's definitely a practical addition.*

The California name came back in 2008 with an unusual Ferrari. The California of today marks a clean break with the past thanks to a number of innovations: an 8-cylinder front engine, manual/automatic dual-clutch transmission, a retractable metal roof (which actually weighs less than a normal canvas roof), multilink rear suspension and direct fuel injection. The engine has a total displacement of 4300 cc and produces 460 hp, the chassis and bodywork are all aluminum and, with its roof up, it has the lowest drag coefficient ever for a Ferrari at 0.32.

Unlike its predecessor, the current California is not one of the most exclusive models from Maranello but it is the cheapest; it was created to increase the company's production by 50%. If its ancestor did not make any concessions to comfort, today's model is the least extreme in the Ferrari line, one which more than any other lends itself to broad use and, by the company's own admission, is more appealing to women.

Many don't even consider it a true Ferrari. The project, in fact, had to take shape under the Maserati name, with the Fiat Group only deciding to use Ferrari's more prestigious "prancing horse" logo when production costs proved too high for the Tridente brand.

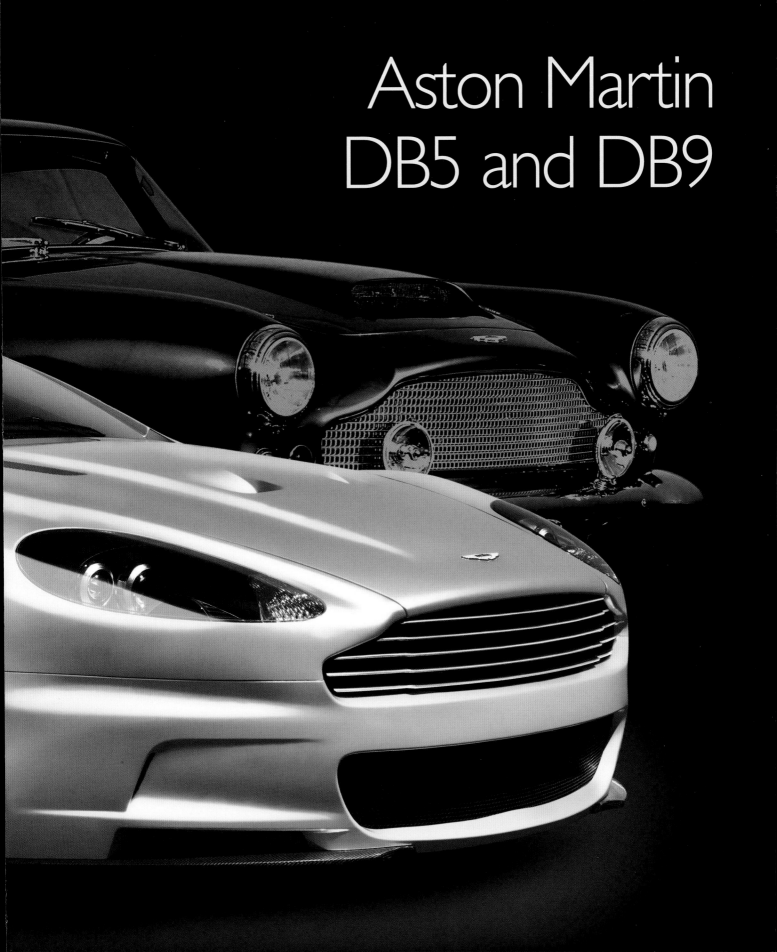

Aston Martin
DB5 and DB9

The essence
of England

Why does this chapter start with the DB5? Because, thanks to its starring role in the 1964 film *Goldfinger*, it is the most famous Aston Martin of all time and was one of the most desired cars of its era. In reality, though, when the DB5 made its first appearance in 1963 it didn't make a big splash, since fans considered it a logical and almost expected evolution of the DB4, whose elegant yet aggressive design had stunned the world at the 1958 Paris Auto Show.

To be as beautiful as it was, the DB4 had help from those who knew a thing or two about good cars. Its aluminum skin was fashioned by the Italian-influenced Touring body shop, which also designed the frame made of thin welded tubes. These two characteristics remained unchanged in the DB5.

The "4" and "5" in the cars' names served to identify the models as the fourth and fifth Aston Martins of the "DB" era. Since 1950, these two letters could be found on everything produced by the company. They were the initials of David Brown, the industrialist from Yorkshire who had bought Aston Martin in 1947 after responding to an anonymous "for sale" listing in the *Times*.

Under the DB4's hood beat an unheard of 6-cylinder, 3.7-liter engine, built at the then new factory in Newport Pagnell. This engine was later increased to 3995 cc and 287 hp, a change that proved to be the sole novelty of the DB5.

In the James Bond movie, a young Sean Connery drove a Silver Birch DB5 with registration BMT 216. The car used for filming, however, was actually a modified DB4 equipped with gadgets like a bulletproof rear window, a rotating license plate that changed numbers and radar. Once shooting was completed, the car remained in the hands of Aston Martin and, after a worldwide promotional tour, was returned to the factory in 1968 stripped of its "tricks" and put up for sale as an ordinary used car. However, a private collector soon identified it, bought it and restored it to its previous condition. Nevertheless, in 1997 the car was stolen and all traces of it have vanished.

The real DB5 in its standard configuration had only a bit part in *Goldfinger*, but it would soon get its own time in the spotlight, accompanying 007 in the adventures *Thunderball* (1965), *GoldenEye* (1995), *Tomorrow Never Dies* (1997) and *Casino Royale* (2006). The car almost was in *The World Is Not Enough* (1999), but unfortunately its scenes ended up on the cutting room floor.

218 top Sean Connery, the most popular 007, poses on the set of Goldfinger *with the Aston Martin DB5. The car is actually a disguised DB4, visible by the covered headlights.*

218 center Among the tricks of the first James Bond Aston Martin were tubes hidden behind the rear lights that scattered oil and nails to escape pursuers. Also, there were spikes affixed to the wheels that could come out and slash the tires on other cars.

218-219 When the DB5 was introduced in 1963 it did not cause a great shock among fans because it was the logical evolution of the DB4, which, however, did surprise fans at the 1958 Paris Auto Show.

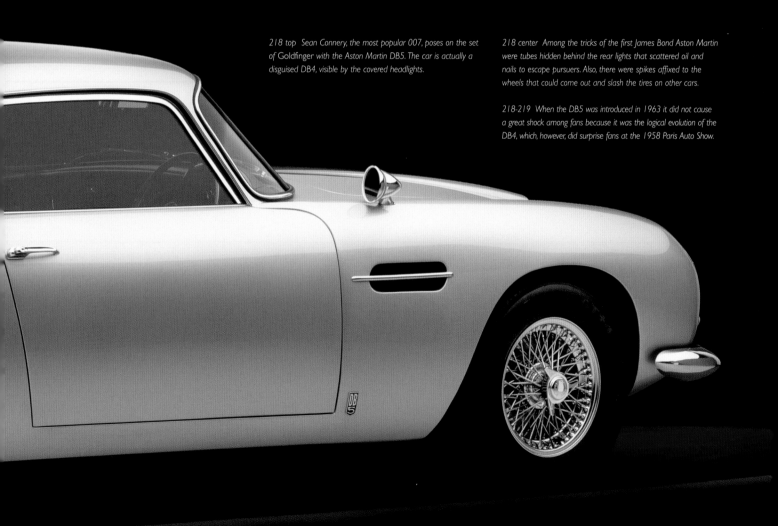

Aside from its close relationship with Bond, the DB5 has also appeared in *Catch Me if You Can* (2002) and *Charlie's Angels: Full Throttle* (2003).

Thanks to the publicity of the James Bond films, the assembly line in the second half of the '60s could barely meet customer demand and 1059 DB5s were sold despite only being in production for two years. This was quite impressive compared to the sales totals of the DB4 (1107 sold) and the DB6, which was the heir to the DB5 and the last Aston Martin with a 6-cylinder engine, of which 1462 were sold. Both of these models had commercial lives nearly twice as long as the DB5.

220-221 Under the hood of the car beat a 6-cylinder, 4000 cc engine with 290 hp, which was a lot of power for the time. Aston Martin remained faithful to this configuration until 1970, when it introduced the first V8.

The muscular snob

The real heir of the DB5, in spirit and in style, arrived 40 years later, at the 2003 Frankfurt Auto Show. It was called the DB9.

But here we take a small detour. Aston Martin's first attempt at a return to the grandeur of the DB4 and DB5 actually dates back to 2001 when the Vanquish was presented. A beautiful coupe designed by Ian Callum, the Vanquish set the stylistic criteria for models that would follow and it mounted, for the first time, a powerful 12-cylinder, 6-liter engine which would be the motor of Aston Martin's rebirth. However, the car was criticized for its automatic transmission, which was not considered up to par with its performance capabilities. Nevertheless, it was immediately appreciated for its luxury and exclusivity and was purchased by many celebrities who considered it an alternative to the Ferrari 575 Maranello.

The handmade Vanquish was produced in small numbers at the historic Newport Pagnell factory, which closed its doors when the last Vanquish left the assembly line in 2007.

Production of the DB9 started in 2004, and in 2005 the convertible version, dubbed the Volante, made its debut.

222-223 The Vanquish. Few cars have had a name as challenging. Its official debut took place at Geneva in 2001 and a year later it became a Bond car in the movie Die Another Day. The car used for filming, though, had a Ford V8 and four-wheel drive.

224-225 The Vanquish introduced a stylistic concept that has been maintained faithfully, not only on the new flagship DB9 but also on the V8 Vantage and other "small" models. This has helped Aston Martin recover after years of crisis that brought it to the brink of closure.

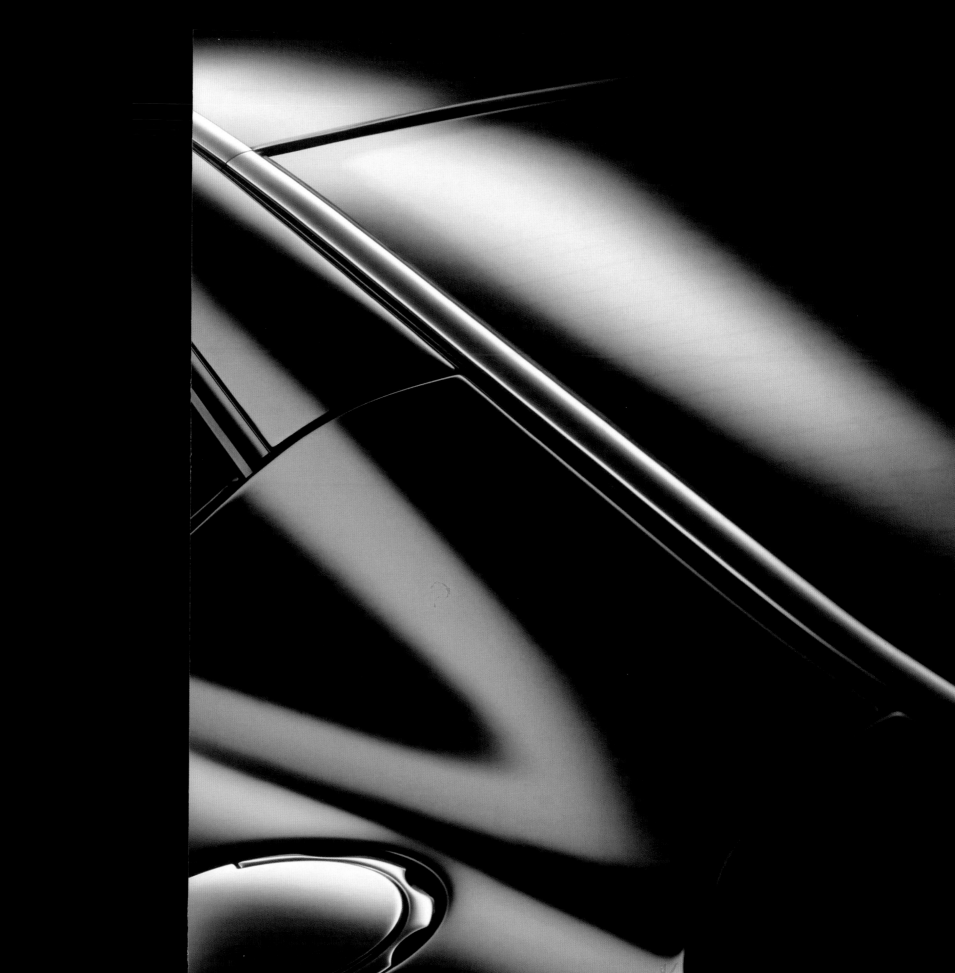

Compared to the DB5, the new car was a beast. The cylinders had doubled to twelve and the power was up to 457 hp. The DB9 was also the first to emerge from the new Aston Martin Gaydon manufacturing plant and the first to use an adjustable aluminum platform bonded by rivets and adhesives. This innovation had been studied by Ford, which owned the English carmaker from 1994 to 2007, as a way to form the basis of different models and free the bodywork of structural tasks, thereby allowing radical stylistic changes with minimal investment.

As beautiful as the DB9 is, the car has strangely made only a few pop culture appearances, the most notable being in *The Fantastic 4* (2005) and the TV series *Desperate Housewives*.

If the DB9 will not be remembered for its "acting" qualities, it will be for its sporting results. It has allowed Aston Martin to return to the highest levels of racing after decades on the sidelines. Unveiled in November 2004, the DB9R racing version won its class in its debut at the Sebring 12 Hours and Silverstone. It would even go on to win the 24 Hours of Le Mans in 2007.

While the DB9R reaped success on the track, the newest road version of the DBS was presented in 2007. It preserved the "skeleton," windows, roof and mechanical base while increasing power up to 510 hp and sporting a much more aggressive look.

The DBS also quickly reestablished itself as James Bond's car, appearing in the film *Casino Royale*

(2006), again before the car was officially on the market, which helped create a buzz. On top of that, pictures of the car used in the shoot were leaked, which allowed the Corgi toy company to exhibit a faithful model at the English Toy Fair in January of '06. Thanks to the Internet, these early shots of the DBS reached every corner of the globe before Aston Martin could release any official promotional photographs.

As per the script of the film, a DBS was destroyed during shooting in a spectacular crash. The remains of this car are now on display in the Gaydon factory in a corridor where other special Aston Martins used by James Bond rest, including the DBS used in the 22nd installment of the Bond story, *Quantum of Solace* (2008). Once again, a car was lost during filming, but this time by mistake. A stunt driver flew off the road and landed in water as he traveled at high speed down a narrow road along Lake Garda.

226-227 The DB9 looks very similar to the Vanquish, but the similarities are only skin deep. The platform is in fact aluminum and it is glued and riveted with aircraft technology. This ensures 25 percent less weight but twice the rigidity than previously obtained, which improves road handling.

BMC Mini and
BMW MINI

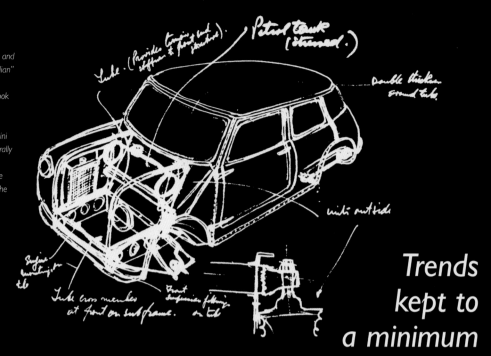

230-231 A black roof, bright red paint and Cooper S written on the hood. The "civilian" version of the racing star of the Monte Carlo Rally in the mid 1960s did not look much different from the standard Mini.

231 top In the first sketches of the Mini one can see the radiator mounted laterally with the engine behind the right front wheel. This unusual position reduces the length of the front end and advances the engine to increase the interior space.

Trends kept to a minimum

Nothing exemplifies the expression "To make virtue out of necessity" like the Mini. After all, the Suez Crisis in 1956 had drastically increased the fuel price, giving rise to a demand for cars that guzzled less gas. So British Motor Company, or BMC, which included the brands Austin, Morris, Riley and Wolseley, asked engineer Alex Issigonis to design a small car that was affordable to buy and, above all, to maintain.

For Issigonis, it was a long-awaited opportunity to put his revolutionary ideas into practice. The only constraint imposed was that he had to use an engine that already existed. This led to the birth of a car with a front engine and front-wheel drive, a combination that was revolutionary at that time. It allowed for small, compact external dimensions (it was a little more than 10 feet, 3 m, long) with enough interior space for four people and luggage. Even the suspension was innovative, with rubber elastic elements instead of the classic softer variety.

The assembly of the body, meanwhile, also utilized extremely economical techniques that helped give the Mini a unique look, one that was as original as its name. Legend has it that the name came from the exclamation of an engineer's wife upon first seeing the car: "It's so mini!"

In keeping with the affordable, essentials-only theme, the interior style was spartan at best. The instrumentation was limited to a single display mounted in the center of the dashboard, and a heating system was offered for a fee.

On August 26, 1959, the car debuted as both the Morris Mini Minor and the Austin Seven, with only minor differences between the two. Sales were sluggish at first, despite the fact that the 496 pound price tag was among the lowest in Great Britain. Soon, however, London's "high society" took notice of the small car, so much so that even the queen wanted to try one, if only as a passenger and with Issigonis driving.

English actor Peter Sellers was so in love with his Mini that he sought to personalize both the interior and exterior with a pattern that resembled woven wicker. He wasn't alone. In the 60's, "Mini-Maniacs" included the Beatles, Brigitte Bardot, Lord Snowdon (husband of England's Princess Margaret), Twiggy (model and symbol of "Swinging London") and even Clint Eastwood.

In the meantime, John Cooper, a manufacturer of racing cars and a friend of Issigonis, had realized the potential of the car and managed to talk BMC into a limited edition 1000-car run with an 848 to 997 cc engine and 34 to 55 hp. This model also used front disc brakes instead of drum brakes.

Launched in 1961, the Cooper was a success and gave rise to the Cooper S, which had a 1071 cc engine and 70 hp. Since 1960 the Mini had been appearing at rallies, and in 1963 Rauno Aaltonen won his class in the Monte Carlo Rally. The following year, Paddy Hopkirk triumphed in the general standings with his red Cooper S, ahead of much more powerful cars.

The feat was repeated in 1966 and 1967. In these years, even Niki Lauda, swayed by the triumphs at Monte Carlo, competed with a Mini.

The small British car was also a winner on the big screen, where, as a star or bit player, it has appeared in hundreds of films. Its most celebrated appearances were in *The Italian Job* (1969) and in *The Bourne Identity* (2002), where a rickety first generation model played a big role in a spectacular chase scene. Many also remember the Mini as the car of choice for TV's Mr. Bean.

The Mini appeared in three James Bond films (*You Only Live Twice*, *The Spy that Loved Me* and *Moonraker*), where the Moke, probably the most unique model of the Mini family, appeared. Created in 1964, this lightweight and fully open model was designed for military use, in particular for helicopter and parachute transportation. It never actually entered into service due to its small wheels and low ground clearance. It had more success in the civilian market, with about 50,000 cars produced.

The Mini was built in Italy by Innocenti between 1965 and 1974 and even had some success in the U.S., where it was sold until 1967, when it was withdrawn following new federal safety standards. This gave rise to the phenomenon of local Mini "re-VIN." Every car has its serial number printed on a metal plate: the VIN, or vehicle identification number. When a Mini was ready to be retired, or disposed, the plate was removed and placed on a twin car purchased abroad. This was done instead of repairing the old Mini, which was exempt from the new standards, by replacing all the parts needed in order to legally drive the car.

Joining the first Mini in 1960 was the station wagon, whose version with exterior wooden panels was most notable; a pair of questionable rear winged, or "tailed," models marketed under the brand names Riley and Wolseley in 1961; and the Clubman, which had a relatively massive front end that lengthened the car by more than 4 inches (11 cm) in 1969. Success continued unabated, and in 1972, 13 years after its debut, the 3 millionth Mini was produced.

Nevertheless, crisis came in the 1980s, as little by little all special versions left production, leaving only the Mini Classic, which was the most faithful

to the original with a 998 cc engine and 40 hp. In 1990, however, a decision was made to reintroduce the Cooper, albeit in a "tamer" version than the original, and the following year the company also debuted a convertible with strange origins: the car began as a modified version hand-built by a German merchant. Because it was so well made, though, the home office eventually acquired the rights and put out roughly 1000 cars between 1991 and 1996.

232 top In the 1969 film The Italian Job, *a group of British criminals use three Minis to steal a great quantity of gold in Turin, making the most of the car's legendary agility.*

232 bottom In the 1990 film Three Men and a Little Lady, *Tom Selleck and Steve Gutenberg are trapped inside a Mini, surrounded by a flock of sheep. The Mini did not have a starring role in this movie, however.*

233 A crowd of people witness one of many attempts involving the Mini to enter the Guinness Book of Records, in this case for the largest number of women in a Mini.

Exaggerated ambitions

234 and 234-235 MINI interior designer Amatino Bruno (top and bottom left) and Director of MINI Design Gert Hildebrand (bottom right) study the interior of the third generation MINI, launched in 2006. There were very few tweaks to style but many changes under the hood. The GP MINI Kit, launched in 2006, has so far been the most extreme version since BMW revived the British car. The engine was increased to 220 hp and the car was 90 pounds (40 kg) lighter thanks to the removal of the rear seats.

235 bottom Exterior designer Marcus Syring also worked on the 2006 MINI. Changes were made to the engines but mostly to the front end, which was elongated to meet safety standards for pedestrians in the event of a collision. The lights were also no longer integrated with the hood and remained fixed when it was open.

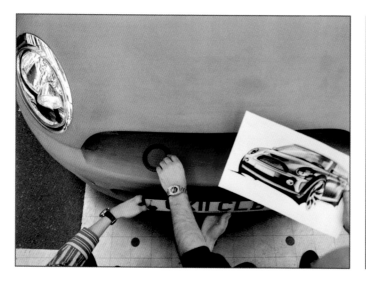

236 top The BMW-era convertible, created in 2004, kept the old engines and body until 2009 when a new version, recognizable by the lack of visible tailgate hinges, was introduced. The car received an additional tool that indicates how long it has been driven with the top down. For many fans, perseverance in this area is a point of honor.

236-237 Unlike the 2004 version, the new convertible has a safety roll bar that only appears when it's needed instead of being fixed. In the event of a rollover, the bars emerge from the tail in a split second. The hood opens electronically in 15 seconds.

237 top *The convertible MINI is also available in a sportier version, the John Cooper Works. It has a 1600 cc turbo engine with 211 hp and the ability to go from 0 to 60 mph (100 km/h) in just 6.9 seconds.*

238-239 *The BMW MINI incorporated many interior elements of the first Mini, like the speedometer mounted in the center of the dashboard instead of behind the steering wheel, instrument graphics, toggle switches and round vents.*

In 2000, after 5.3 million cars had been made, production was finally stopped to make room for a new model. The seeds for this new version were planted in 1994 when BMW acquired the brand. From then on, MINI would be written in capital letters. In 1997 at the Frankfurt Auto Show the company presented the ACV 30 prototype, which led to the definitive version released in 2000.

Compared to the Mini of Alex Issigonis, this car had completely different mechanics, larger engines (1400-1600 cc), luxury fittings, higher prices and much bigger dimensions. However, the exterior and interior design made it immediately recognizable as a child of the original idea. The British spirit had survived despite German ownership and engines made outside Europe. The gasoline engines were produced in a Brazilian factory through a joint venture between BMW and Chrysler, while the diesel engines were provided by Toyota.

Not long after, the Cooper was reborn, with the Cooper S in 2002, a convertible version in 2005 and the station wagon – called Clubman, even if the old Clubman was originally a sedan – in 2007. With a moderate restyling that took place in 2006, the company decided to also replace the engines, which had not been particularly noteworthy for consumption or performance. The new engines were produced in collaboration with Peugeot and Citroën and offered a much better performance.

In 2008 a small fleet of 450 was produced for the electric market in California, while 2010 saw the arrival of the SUV version – the Countryman – which was also offered with four-wheel drive.

Following a legend, even the MINI of the BMW era quickly became a trendy, iconic car, quickly earning spots in television series like *NCIS, Special Squad Cobra 11* and *Commissione Cordier* and films such as *Austin Powers - Goldmember* (2001) and the remake of *The Italian Job* (2003).

A star, as they say, was born.

240 top Like the station wagon version of the '60s, the Clubman has a curious double-hinged tailgate which requires the presence of two small wipers. Rear visibility is affected, but it's details like this that make the car unique.

240-241 The door opening system is another one of the Clubman's oddities. On the left side there is only the front door. On the right, however, there is also a small rear door that is rear-hinged and facilitates access to the back seats.

241 top With the arrival of BMW, the MINI received a diesel engine for the first time in its history. Initially it was a 1400 cc from Toyota, but now the car uses a 1600 cc diesel engine made by Peugeot that provides enough power for the small station wagon at full load.

Jaguar Mark 2 and S-Type

As fast and aggresive as a cat

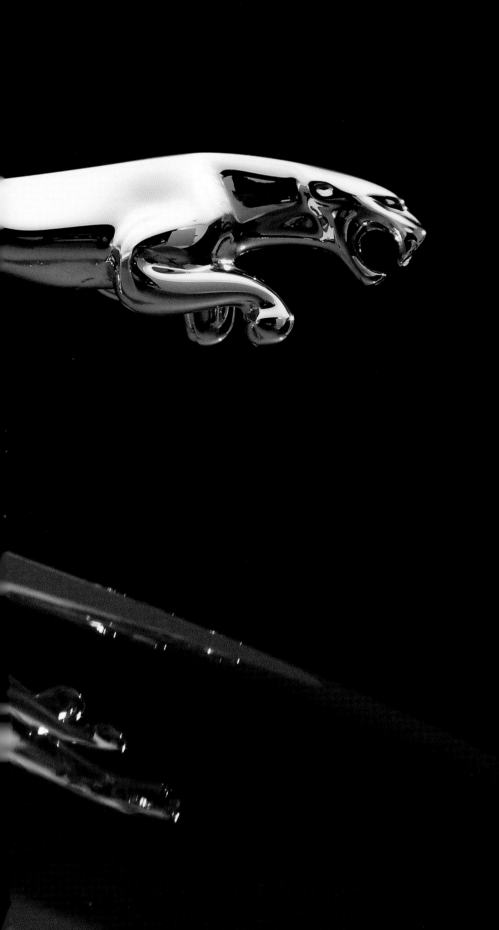

"Grace, space, pace." This has always been the Jaguar creed, one applied not only to its world-famous roadsters and coupes but also to its sedans.

With the 1955 Mark 1, the Coventry carmaker began exploring the sports sedan segment of the market but didn't take it as far as it could have. The car had underwhelming performance and undersized drum brakes. When it came time to improve the project, Jaguar engineers had one chance and they could not fail.

The Mark 2, which represented a substantial evolution of the Mark 1, was presented in 1959. Compared to its predecessor, the Mark 2 was radically changed, both aesthetically and mechanically. The restyling of the body focused on a redesign of the doors, an increase of the glass surfaces, a reconfigured tail which made the car leaner and, to a lesser extent, a reshaped front end. The interior was also redone, especially the dashboard, instrumentation and seats. The results were surprising. Although it was officially only a "revisiting" of the Mark 1, the Mark 2 had now managed a new elegance that transformed it into a timeless example of style.

On the mechanical side, the Mark 2 signaled the arrival of disc brakes, while the 2.4 liter engine, which was considered the main culprit of the Mark 1's poor performance, went from 112 hp to 120 hp. Twin engines that were between 3.4 and 3.8 liters and had 210 and 220 hp, respectively, were still available for the most insatiable Jaguar fans.

244-245 The "jaguar" only appeared after 1945 when the British carmaker changed its name from Swallow Sidecar Company to Jaguar. In many countries, the famous feline statuette on the hood has been banned for security reasons.

However, the car still used an in-line 6-cylinder engine – the architecture that had made Jaguar's name and which remained unchanged until the late '90s. The Mark 2 was a success, selling almost 84,000 units in eight years, a remarkably high number for a car so expensive and "elitist." As a true sports sedan, the Mark 2 also raced successfully in the European Touring Car Championship. The downside to all this was its popularity in the underworld. Thanks to its reputation as a brilliant and spacious car – the most powerful version could carry five adults and go from 0 to 60 in less than nine seconds, exceeding 124 mph (200 km/h) – the Mark 2 was often the car of choice for criminals, so much so that even the British police had to adopt it to patrol highways.

The Mark 2's subtle exterior hid its superior acceleration and drivability. In the 1960s it was often dubbed "the perfect Q-car," a term inspired by the "Q-ships" and vessels of the two World Wars that were armed to the teeth to battle submarines but looked like simple merchant ships.

This stealthy image earned the car many cinematic appearances, often in detective films. However, it wasn't limited to gumshoe work. In 1967 the Mark 2 was renamed the 240 or 340, according to displacement, and certain characteristic and expensive features, like spoked wheels, excessive chrome and leather interiors, were dropped. This extended the car's commercial life for a couple years by lowering its price. This cost cutting tactic was used to eliminate the overlap with the S-Type in 1963 which, in fact, reused much of the mechanics and body but was ranked in a higher class.

246-247 Massive bumpers, such as those seen here, help identify Mark 2s built before 1967. Since then, more subtle bumpers were adopted, the 3800 cc engine was dropped and the versions with 2400 cc and 3400 cc engines were rechristened Jaguar 240 and Jaguar 340.

247 top The Mark 2, especially the version with the more powerful 3.8 engine, was used by the British police. In the '60s, English highways did not post speed limits and fast cars were needed to patrol them. The problem was that criminals often used the same car.

248-249 The spoked wheels were expensive but gave a clear touch of class. In the last years of production, however, cheaper stamped steel rims were standard when this model was repositioned to make the Jaguar more accessible.

Last appeal to the past

Even after production ceased, the Mark 2 remained in the hearts of fans as a Jaguar icon, along with the E-type coupe and roadster, and directly inspired the new S-Type, which was presented at the 1998 Birmingham Auto Show at a time when the company was struggling to recover its identity.

The car, which went into production at the beginning of the following year, was a sedan of medium to large dimensions with rear-wheel drive, powerful engines and strong stylistic bonds with its ancestor thanks to the four round headlights and the shape of the grill, hood, tail and front end.

Although built at the Castle Bromwich factory, the S-Type had American roots, as Ford had bought Jaguar in 1989 and had designed a mechanical base for not only the British sedan but also the Lincoln LS

250-251 Among the various versions of the S-Type, the sportiest was the "R" which, when it was presented, earned the title of fastest sedan ever produced by Jaguar thanks to a 4200 cc supercharged V8 that delivered 395 hp. Aesthetically, it was distinguished by a "honeycomb" mask used in place of the traditional vertical strips.

and Ford Thunderbird. The same platform, although shortened, was even supposed to be be used for the 2005 Ford Mustang but the American carmaker decided to drop Jaguar and the project stalled. The Indian group Tata later purchased the brand in 2008.

The S-Type nevertheless had a lot of hidden components derived from Ford. This included a new 3-liter, 6-cylinder engine which marked Jaguar's re-turn to this engine configuration, although the cylinders were layed out in a V instead of in line.

The restyling in late 2002 provided an opportunity to correct some flaws, especially the reliability of the electronics, and enrich the engine range with, among other things, an 8-cylinder turbocharged engine meant for the sporty S-Type R. Finally, in 2004 the "sacrilegious," at least according to the Jaguar tradition, turbodiesel arrived.

The S-Type, which eventually gave way to the far less nostalgic XF in 2008, did not have the Mark 2's luck on the screen. In fact, the car has made only a few appearances in TV series like *The Sopranos* and *Desperate Housewives*. Nevertheless, because of its favorable balance between price, quality and image, it is today playing a leading role in the used car market.

Ford Mustang

The "pony car" par excellence

254 top *The 1969 movie Bullitt, which featured Steve McQueen and a Mustang GT, won an Oscar for Best Editing. The main chase scene is still regarded as one of the best of its kind.*

254-255 *The Mustang was a huge success in 1964, its first year of production, thanks to the excellent value of the 6- and 8-cylinder engines. Among the options were air conditioning and rear safety belts, which were then rare.*

22,000 units sold on the day of its presentation, 100,000 (which happened to be the sales goal for the entire year) in the first three months and 418,812 in the first twelve months. These cold, hard numbers are more than enough to show the incredible success that the Ford Mustang achieved upon its launch in 1964. This glory was anything but short-lived. By the end of 1966 there were one million Mustangs registered and, after five generations and nearly fifty years on the market, the number of Mustangs produced has exceeded five million. For a sports car that would normally be restricted to a limited market, that is a sensational number.

The Ford Mustang is the only "pony car" (starting with the Chevrolet Corvair in 1959, this typically American category includes cars that are fast and powerful but relatively inexpensive) to have remained in production without interruption until today.

Built on the Falcon sedan's platform in both coupe and convertible versions, it took its name from a celebrated fighter aircraft from the Second World War – the P-51 Mustang – and was inspired by the famous horse of the American West, an animal known for its grace, strength and speed.

The first model left the assembly line on March 9, 1964 and was shown to the public on April 17 at the Universal Exhibition in New York. The project, developed in only 18 months, was directly supervised by Lee Iacocca, Ford's president from 1964 to 1978, who set the stylistic guidelines. The car was to have four seats instead of two to attract as many customers as possible; an overall weight less than 2500 pounds (1100 kg); a maximum length of less than 181 inches (460 cm), even though the car actually measured 182 inches; and a list price under $2,500. Despite these restrictions, the car also had to be powerful, comfortable and luxurious.

The Mustang's legendary status was quickly cemented, not only for its impressive sales numbers but also for its "extracurricular" activities. One month after its unveiling, a Mustang was the official pace car of the Indianapolis 500, and four months later it made its debut on the big screen in *Goldfinger*.

In 1965, the version produced by Carroll Shelby, which still marks the most powerful Mustang, made its appearance. The first series of this mod-

er boasted a 4700 cc V8 engine with 308 hp and 360 hp in the racing version. The car was also painted exclusively in black and had no rear seats. One of these Shelbys, a 1967 Shelby GT 500 affectionately nicknamed "Eleanor," was the star of the movie *Gone in 60 Seconds* (2000).

However, when one thinks about the Mustang and Hollywood, the first thought is probably *Bullitt* (1968), where a Highland green GT fastback with a modified 325 hp engine accompanied Steve Mc-

Queen on his adventures. In the 2000s two versions of the celebrated model from that film surfaced. However, neither exceeded the original's power.

The first Mustang series, which in Germany was sold as a T-5 Mustang since the name Mustang was used by a lawn mower factory, remained on the market for about ten years. In that time it continuously grew in size and weight. Consequently, when the oil crisis arose and cus-

256-257 The Boss 302 version (pictured here is a 1970 model with equipment created by Danny Moore and Jerry Crew) included a powerful 290 hp V8 engine, and it achieved great success on the track. The most important victory was undoubtedly in the Trans-Am Championship in 1970 with Parnelli Jones behind the wheel.

tomers demanded lower fuel consumption, forcing the disappearance of rivals like the Plymouth Barracuda, AMC Javelin and Dodge Challenger, Ford built a new, more stripped down model which was more consistent with the original.

For the second generation in 1974, the platform of the compact Pinto was used, the convertible version vanished and, for the first time, 4-cylinder engines were used, the least powerful of which had only 88 hp. Despite being smallejr,

however, the weight was increased to meet safety and emissions regulations, a combination that caused performance to dip. Even the road handling was inferior to past standards. Despite these flaws, sales remained strong.

The third Mustang, produced from 1979 to 1993, with a convertible version now back on the market, offered a squarer style, larger trunk and more room for rear passengers. Sales, however, dropped sharply to about 100,000 units per

year, forcing the company to consider replacing it with a model based on the platform of the Mazda MX-6. As these plans leaked, however, Mustang fans opposed the idea, as this would have not only meant a move to front-wheel drive but would have also ruled out a V8 engine. Fearing a commercial flop, the bosses in Detroit abandoned the project and decided instead to lengthen the life of the existing model with a heavy restyling.

Back to its roots

Sales improved slightly with the 1994 launch of the fourth generation, which now included 6- and 8-cylinder engines and featured a rounder, more muscular style. But it was not until the fifth series, presented at the 2004 Detroit Auto Show, that the Mustang once again won the hearts of fans.

Less than 189 inches (480 cm) long and with V6 and V8 engines from 3700 to 5400 liters, the new Mustang has a "retro-futurist" style directly inspired by the original of the '60s. It's not just the styling that's closely connected with the past. Even the marketing strategy is the same, since the Ford coupe today boasts one of the best balances between price and performance.

But if the Mustang once attracted young American drivers (in its first years on the market, 70% of its buyers did not have a car to offer as exchange) it now mostly attracts a nostalgic audience, one yearning for decades that passed long ago but remain in the heart and mind.

258-259 Many engineers, designers and workers have tried their luck on the Mustang. One of the most popular is Jack Roush, who has worked on the Ford sports car since 1988. The 2001 Stage 3 distinguished itself from the standard models with a 360 hp V8 engine, larger wheels and a new front bumper.

Alfa Romeo Spider

The global heartthrob

The convertible version of the Giulia was unveiled at the Geneva Auto Show in March 1966 and was, at that time, still simply called the Spider 1600. In the meantime, however, Alfa had launched a competition for a new name. More than 140,000 responses, including 15,000 from outside Italy, were collected by dealerships, with "Duetto" (or "Duet"), suggested by Guidobaldo Trionfi of Brescia, coming out on top. Trionfi won a Spider for his winning entry.

But almost immediately a problem arose. That name was already used for a snack sold by the confectioner Pavesi, so just a year after unveiling the car Alfa had to abandon it. Nevertheless, the name had become so successful that until production ended in 1994 the public continued to affectionately call the car "Duetto."

The naming competition was not the only way the commercial launch was promoted. In 1966, three Spiders were loaded onto the deck of the *Raffaello* ocean liner, where passengers could also see the car in motion, and taken to New York. Perhaps more importantly, the Spider was Dustin Hoffman's car in the movie *The Graduate* (1967), which helped win the hearts of Americans for whom the car would remain "The Graduate."

In 1968, the 1600 version made way for the 1300 Junior and 1750 Veloce. Both, however, had short careers, as just a year later Alfa launched the second generation of the Spider with a redesigned tail that shed the characteristic "cuttlefish bone" design. The new configuration had the advantage of increasing the cargo capacity, but it also veered from what was perhaps the last stylistic project directly supervised by Battista Pininfarina, who had designed the body. Another major change was made in 1971 with the arrival of a 2000 cc engine.

In 1978, the Giulia, which supplied the Spider's engines, transmissions and suspensions, went out of production to make room for the new, completely different Giulietta. The Spider, however, continued to be built with the original dated mechanics, which nevertheless still pleased customers.

In 1983 , however, it was time for a facelift, one that involved massive changes to the interior, front end and tail. The wraparound bumpers were now much more pronounced and a striking black rubber spoiler was now included. The difference from the 1966 design was even more noticeable in 1990 when the tail was again modified to give it a modern look, but one that also failed to mesh with the rest of the car, which continued to maintain a '60s vibe and still was a hit with nostalgics. By then, the U.S. absorbed most of the Alfa Spiders produced, and when the company decided to withdraw from that market in 1994 production of the car ceased. This was the last Alfa Romeo with rear-wheel drive until the advent of the 8C, which came thirteen years later.

Challenging a bulky past

Nevertheless, by autumn 1994 Alfa previewed two new sports cars at the Paris Auto Show: the GTV coupe and its convertible derivative, which took the Spider name. These cars had a muscular and edgy style, which was still designed by Pininfarina, and mechanics derived from the 155, which meant there were many Fiat touches and innovations, since Fiat had absorbed Alfa in 1986. First among these were the transverse engine and front-wheel drive.

The design was immediately pleasing to the eye, as was its the car's aggressiveness, originality and road handling, which still reflected the Turin influence but leaned on it a little less.

Production began in 1995 and initially the car came with two engines: a 2000 cc 4-cylinder with 150 hp and a 3000 cc 6-cylinder with 192 hp. The latter was designed for a return to the U.S. market, but that never materialized. During a career that lasted until 2005, 1800 cc, 2000 cc turbo and 3200 cc 6-cylinder engines all were produced.

Since this kind of car did not have the public attention it did in the '60s and '70s, the design and interior only underwent modifications in 1998 and 2003, with Alfa limiting its efforts in this niche market and choosing to focus on more profitable models.

This did not prevent Alfa from bringing back the Spider in 2006, with the design this time derived from the Brera coupe unveiled a year earlier. Curiously, while that version was designed by Giugiaro, the transformation into a Spider was overseen by Pininfarina.

The design of the car made an immediate impact, so much so that only a few days after the debut at the Geneva Auto Show the Spider was awarded the title of "2006 Cabrio of the Year" by a panel of experts.

The mechanics of the car are similar to the 159 sedan and are mainly the result of the collaboration between Fiat and General Motors between 2000 and 2005. Initially there were two engines available: a 2000 and 3200 6-cylinder, the latter of which also included four-wheel drive. In 2007, a 2400 turbodiesel version was introduced. In an effort to revitalize sales, which had never really taken off due to high prices, limited performance caused by the car's elevated weight and engines that were not really Alfa's style, the 1750 turbo gas engine and an economical 2000 turbo diesel were introduced in 2009.

Aside from being a fine example of Italian style, the Spider of today is far more comfortable, refined and full of its predecessor's '60s spirit, even if the freshness and simplicity of the old "Duetto" will indelibly remain in the hearts of Alfisti and convertible lovers.

264-265 After a less than successful experience with the 1994 Spider, Alfa reworked the third edition in 2006. This model was derived from the beautiful Brera coupe designed by Giugiaro, but

265 top From its official presentation at the Geneva Auto Show, the latest generation of the Spider was much loved for its compact and sleek design. In a few days it was voted 2006 "Cabrio of the Year." The mechanical base was that of the 159 sedan.

265 center Compared to the "Duetto," the 2006 Spider was much more comprehensive in scope and refined technically, since it was now also available with all-wheel drive and a diesel engine. But many fans still miss the simplicity of its predecessor.

Chevrolet Camaro

Low cost and lots of fun

The laws of the marketplace are clear: without competition, a product likely will never improve. It isn't a coincidence that in the United States, Ford and General Motors both reached their apex when their rivalry was at its most intense, between 1950 and 1973.

The Chevrolet Camaro is an icon of the "pony car," as reasonably priced sports cars are sometimes called in America. It was born right in the middle of this market war. In 1963 Ford launched the Mustang and sold over 100,000 in the first six months, forcing Chevrolet to scramble for a response.

The engineers immediately began work on the XP-836 project and the definitive version was officially unveiled on September 12, 1966. Choosing a name was a long process, with Nova, Panther, Chaparral and Wildcat all taken into consideration. Even GeMini, which was a play on the GM initials, was suggested, but the company preferred a little more distance from the overall brand in the event that the car flopped.

Camaro, which in old French means "friend" or "companion," initially provoked derision from many, especially when it was discovered that in Spanish

"camaron" means "shrimp." Those laughing, however, were soon silenced by the quality of the car.

The first generation was available in both a coupe or a roadster version. Much of the mechanics came from the Pontiac Firebird. The engines varied between 6 and 8 cylinders and had a displacement between 4.1 and 6.5 liters, while the interior included two rear seats, even though they were for "emergency use only."

The general public soon grew fond of the Camaro, which was winning on U.S. race tracks while at the same time being available for purchase at dealerships down the street. In those days, decisions on products usually came quickly and the Chevrolet brass soon renewed the Camaro. The second generation of the car was unveiled in 1970. At the same time, the convertible version disappeared from the scene while sizes and overall weight grew, with the V6 and V8 engines ranging between 3.8 and 7.4 liters

The 1974 oil crisis massacred the "pony car" segment of the market and severely damaging Chevrolet's competition, so much so that for the first time in its history there were more registered Camaros on the road than Mustangs in 1977.

The third generation Camaro arrived in 1982, characterized by square headlights and a full line of innovations such as fuel injection, a four-speed automatic transmission (a five-speed manual was also available), 16-inch (40 cm) wheels and a practical hatchback. The weight decreased, the convertible roadster returned and a four-cylinder engine, unusually small by American standards at only 2.5 liters, was introduced.

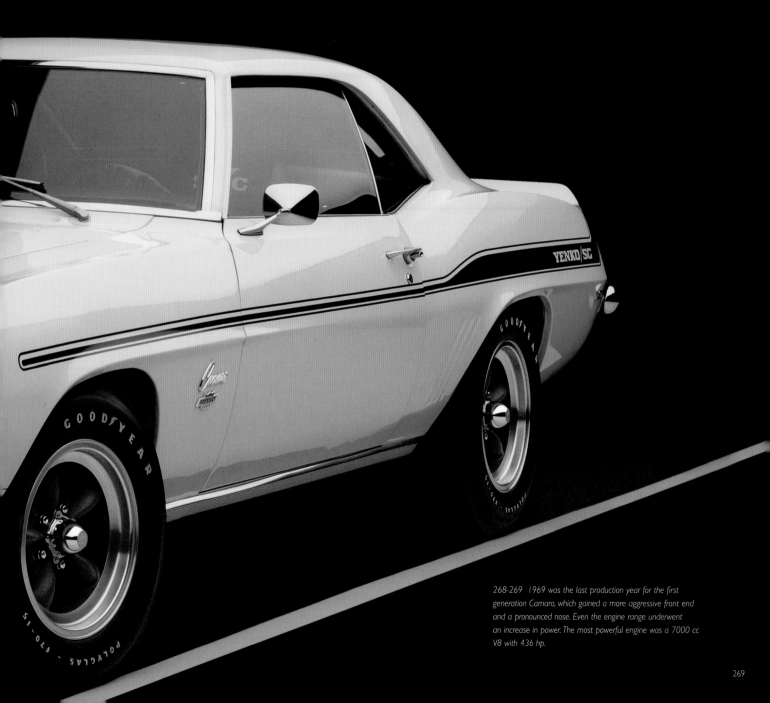

268-269 1969 was the last production year for the first generation Camaro, which gained a more aggressive front end and a pronounced nose. Even the engine range underwent an increase in power. The most powerful engine was a 7000 cc V8 with 436 hp.

Not loved in Europe

With the passage of time, the Camaro lost the appeal that it once had. The fourth generation, produced from 1993 to 2002, was also available in Europe. But generally speaking, sports cars are not as attractive to the mass public as they once were, even if the myth of the car was now firmly entrenched, as evidenced by a lyric in one of Pearl Jam's most famous songs, 1998's "Wishlist" – "I wish I was the full moon shining off your Camaro's hood."

270-271 The fourth series of the Chevrolet sports car was sold in its first two years of production with only two engines: a 3400 6-cylinder version with 162 hp and a 5700 V8 with 275 hp. General Motors made a fruitless attempt to import this model to Europe. In 1993, the sporty Z28 had the honor of being used as the official pace car of the Indianapolis 500.

271

For the legendary Camaro – which has appeared in movies such as *Christine* (1983), *Charlie's Angels* (2000) and in TV series like *Miami Vice*, *The X-Files* and *Dukes of Hazzard* – it seemed like the end. But thanks to another film, *Transformers* (2007), the desire for the Chevrolet "pony car" was rekindled.

In that Michael Bay movie, a yellow 1976 model turns into a shiny version of the prototype presented at the 2006 Detroit Auto Show. However, it took another three years for that car to become a reality and Americans could finally buy the new Camaro with both 6- and 8-cylinder engines and a displacement ranging from 3.5 to 6.2 liters.

It is not known whether the car will be officially imported into Europe, but some models are trickling in through independent dealers. Of course, it doesn't help that American sports cars have always attracted little interest in the Old World, mostly because of their large engines and high fuel consumption. However, the rebirth of the Camaro could be a sign of hope. Maybe the moon described by Pearl Jam is returning to shine on Detroit, much the way it did when Chevrolet and Ford battled to offer the best products possible.

272-273 and 273 The current Camaro debuted on the big screen before it made it to dealerships. However, the yellow model that appeared in the 2007 Transformers movie was in fact a Pontiac GTO on which the body of the 2006 Camaro Concept was transplanted. In addition, for the robot Bumblebee, who was the car's alter ego in the film, pieces of a Volkswagen Beetle were used.

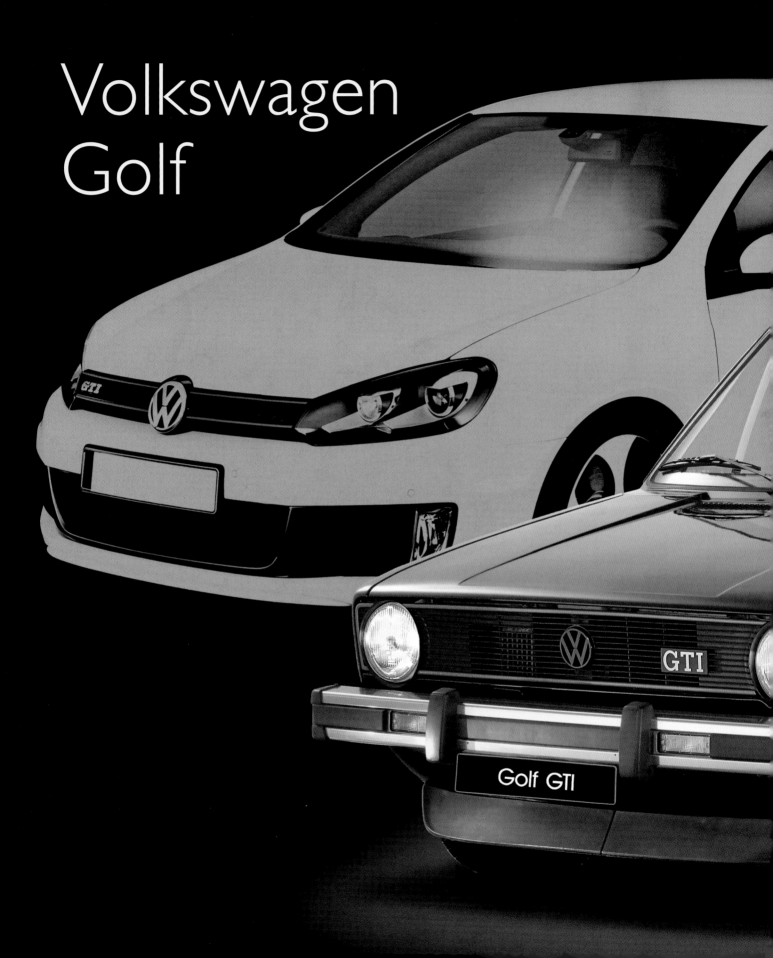

Volkswagen Golf

The compact that changed everything

"The Golf is always the Golf." In good times and bad, this is the essence of a car that some have accused of lacking innovation but which nevertheless set a style and has remained loyal to it since 1974 through six generations of models. In that time, it has become a trusted name for millions of motorists.

To prove there's value to Volkswagen's conservative approach, just look at this staggering sales figure: unveiled in 1974, a million units had already been produced just two years later. That impressive production continued unabated, reaching 5 million cars produced by 1982, 10 million by 1988 (Golf II), 15 million by 1994 (Golf III), 20 million by 2000 (Golf IV) and 25 million by 2007 (Golf V). This success was so massive, in fact, that in June of 2002 Golf number 21,517,415 left the assembly line, surpassing the production record of its most illustrious ancestor, the Beetle.

When the first Golf, designed by Giorgetto Giugiaro, appeared it stunned the general public. The car was spacious, modern, economical and discreet enough to not be adopted by any particular ideology, which was not an easy thing to avoid. Most of all, the car was extremely gratifying. The first Golf was a very well-crafted car, subtly sporty in style and thoroughly equipped and comfortable on the inside, so much so that drivers tended to forget that the engine only offered 1100 cc and 50 hp.

But all was not rosy, at least from the standpoint of some reviewers who felt that the Golf represented Volkswagen's identity crisis, as the company had been painstakingly trying to distance itself from the Beetle. Nevertheless, the Golf's success surpassed the most optimistic forecasts. The car was embraced by the general public, an acceptance facilitated by the aura of indestructibility inherited from the Beetle, and eventually defined a new car category — the affordable compact sedan, accessible to everyone.

276 The first design of the Golf series, produced from 1974 to 1983, was the work of Giugiaro and was immediately popular for its rationality and elegance. For Volkswagen, which was set to replace the obsolete Beetle, this was a real revolution.

276-277 The style of the Golf, which still remains, hit its peak in 1976 when the GTI version was presented. The exterior was distinguished by a front end outlined in red and a few other details, but its 1600 cc 110 hp engine allowed it to keep up with more renowned sports cars.

Golf GTI

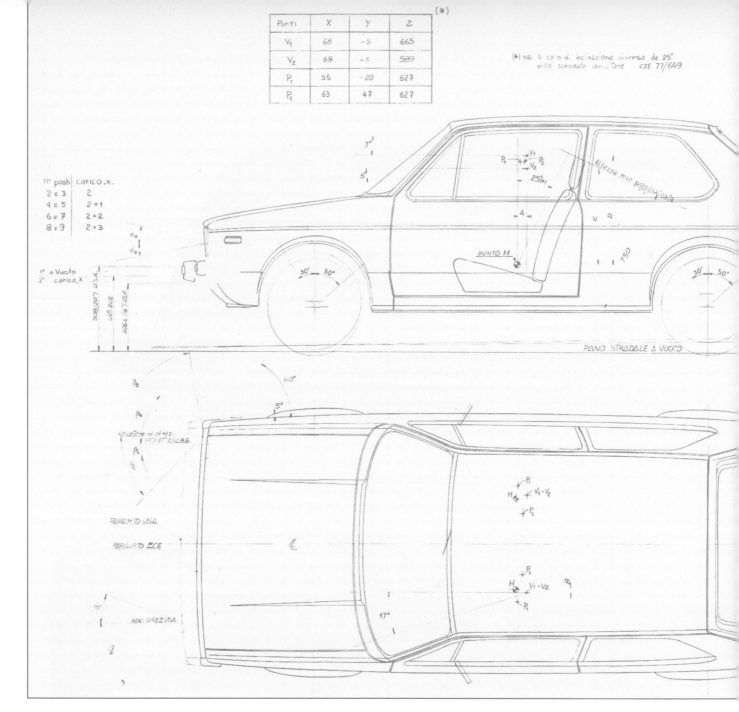

Punti	X	Y	Z
V1	68	-5	665
V2	68	-5	589
P1	35	-20	627
P2	63	47	627

Eventually it would become the benchmark in its class, a standard other companies were forced to chase.

1983 saw the arrival of the Golf II, which represented a leap forward compared to the competition. It maintained the proportions of the first series but was more modern and aerodynamic, meaning rounded corners and windows fitted flush with the bodywork. Furthermore, depending on the version and equipment, it boasted a range of options un-

usual for its class, starting with a 16-valve engine, a volumetric compressor, all-wheel drive, digital instrumentation, air conditioning and power windows, even for the rear passengers.

The '90s, however, brought on a period of crisis for the Golf. The first European emissions regulations limited the performance of the thrusters, while the new design of the 1991 Golf III was considered less elegant and somewhat sterile compared with previous generations. Moreover, in-

creased industrial costs and a change in production strategies had an impact on the car's quality standards, with the finishing now not as obviously above average for its class. However, despite relatively high prices, even this generation of the Golf sold well. It kept some of the basics of the Golf I and II, especially with regard to the rigorous design process and practicality of the vehicle, which acted as a sort of guarantee of reliability for the car and the company that produced it.

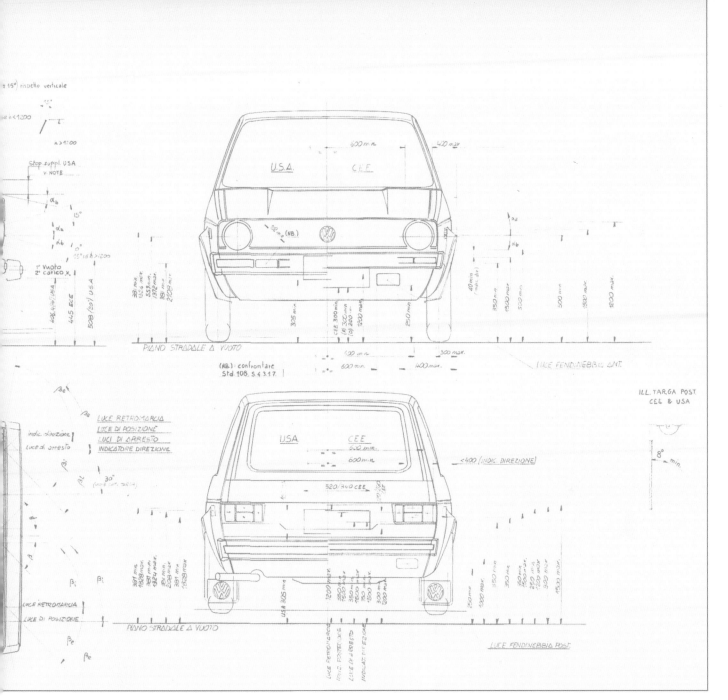

However, the Golf III soon ran into its biggest problem at seemingly the peak of Volkswagen's success. Even though it was voted "Car of the Year" in 1992 and 1994, the Golf, Europe's best-selling car for 13 consecutive years, lost the top spot to the Fiat Punto. Thus, the Golf III was sent into retirement after just six years of production.

1997 saw the arrival of the Golf IV, a much more classic looking version that reproduced and refined stylistic concepts from the original model.

The finishing in the interior was of a higher quality, so much so that it is regarded by many as the best Golf ever built despite receiving some inevitable criticism regarding the rear seating space and cargo capacity (not exactly small defects for a supposed family car) and the effectiveness of the rear suspension. Still, it allowed Volkswagen to regain the leadership of the European market, even if the Golf's prices at that point had risen well above the average for its category.

278-279 The first Golf was 12.5 feet (4 meters) long and weighed under a ton (900 kg), so its dimensions were not much bigger than the small economy cars of today. It was, however, spacious, practical and suitable for families. It soon became the car for those who wanted to distance themselves from the overly austere image of the compact sedans of the '70s. It was available in three and five door versions, and a convertible was released in 1979.

*Changing
without
getting lost*

In 2003, the fifth Golf series arrived with a more muscular style and increased dimensions, partly to counteract past criticisms about passenger space. The design was more modern and the mechanics were largely inherited from its cousin, the Audi A3, which had been unveiled only a short time earlier. This sharing of engines, suspensions and platforms with other models from the ownership group (like the Golf's older sister, the Passat, but also the Seat Leon and Skoda Octavia) allowed a significant reduction in production costs, which had gone through the roof with the fourth generation.

Throughout its commercial life, numerous technical innovations were introduced, such as direct injection diesel engines with the original injector pump system and a twin supercharged injection system for gasoline engines.

The VI series, presented at the end of 2008 and still in production today, is the result of a thorough reinterpretation of the previous generation, even if the aesthetic differences are hardly noticeable on first glance. With this version the company introduced a new front end for the car, a shape that would be progressively carried over to the rest of the Volkswagen product line; at the time it had been adopted by the Polo and Touareg. The technical side saw the introduction of a turbo diesel common rail direct injection system rather than the injector pump, which had proved too complex and costly; an "intelligent" suspension that regulated the structure of the car; an automatic parking system; and a manual/automatic dual-clutch transmission, among other items.

Built as a 3- or 5-door sedan, the Golf has, in the course of its long career, seen convertible, station wagon and minivan versions. But the most evocative version, the one that acted as the driving force for global sales, was the sporty GTI.

280 top The Golf is a worldwide success built not only in Europe (shown is the German plant in Wolfsburg) but also in Brazil, China and South Africa. In June 2002, global production exceeded that of the legendary Beetle, with car No 21,517,415 leaving the assembly line.

280-281 This model is a GTI from the fifth series, sold from 2003 to 2008, which shared a mechanical base with the Audi A3. Compared to the fourth series, it had large dimensions and a more solid appearance, which allowed a considerable increase in passenger and cargo space.

The first version, which had a 1600 cc, 110 hp engine and weighed just over 1750 pounds (800 kg), dates back to 1976. It featured unprecedented performance for its time thanks to a power-to-weight ratio that remained unbeaten for many years. It invented the notion of a car as a "little bomb," an idea for a medium-sized coupe that won the hearts of young drivers. The Golf GTI II was the first car with a wide circulation to mount an engine with four valves per cylinder, which would eventually be increased to five in the GTI IV series. The power of the Golf GTI has been progressively increased over the years, reaching 230 hp for the 2006 30th anniversary version that was produced in a limited run.

Given its widespread distribution, the Golf has appeared countless times on the small and big screens but strangely has never really played a starring role in any of these, outside of purely automotive-themed productions. Evidently, it's enough to be an A-list star where it really counts — in sales.

282-283 and 283 The sixth generation Golf, which debuted in 2008, was designed by the Italian Walter de' Silva, who works with Alfa Romeo and is Volkswagen's head of design, in a way that seemed to reestablish a link back to the first series of Giugiaro. These striking images show the stages of storage for a newly produced Golf at the CarTower Autostadt distribution center, built near the factory in Wolfsburg. On average there are 550 cars delivered to customers daily.

Bibliography

Alberts, Gino, Evangelisti, Athos. *Porsche - History of a Legend*. Porsche, Italy.
Alfa Romeo. *All the models of the Novecento*. Domus.
Alfieri, B., Bernardet, J., Molineri, G., Alberts, G. *Giugiaro Design*. Automobilia.
Altorio, Enzo. *The Fiat Nuova 500*. Automitica.
Antonick, Michael. *Corvette*. MBI.
Austen, Jörg, Walter, Sigmund. *Porsche 911 - Evolution and Technique*. Giorgio Nada.
Batazzi, Mark. *Volkswagen Beetle*. Nada.
Carroll, J. *Classic Jeeps - The Jeep from World War II to the Present Day*. Motorbooks International.
Clemens, Kevin. *Thirty Years of the Volkswagen Golf & Rabbit*. Iconografix.
Dowsey, David. *Aston Martin - Power, Beauty and Soul*. Peleus Press.
Felicioli, Richard P. *Fiat: Creativity, Design, Success*. Automobilia.
Fiat. *1899–1999: All the Fiats*. Domus.
Fiat. *Models of the Twentieth Century*. Domus.
Flammang, James M. *Chrysler Chronicle*. Publications International.
Michael, Frostick. *Rolls Royce: The Whole Story*. Automobilia.
Golding, Rob. *Mini Thirty-Five Years Old*. Osprey.
Jaguar. *Jaguar Mk I & Mk 2 1955–1969, Brooklands Road Test Portfolio*. Brooklands Books.
Langworth, Richard. *Mercedes Benz: The First Hundred Years*. Beekman House.
Massaro, Sergio. *Ferrari: A Legend*. Giunti.
Meikle, Jeffrey L. *Twentieth Century Limited: Industrial Design in America 1925–1939*. Temple University.

Newhardt, David. *Mustang*. Motorbooks International.
Paxton, Mark. *Citroen 2CV: The Essential Buyer's Guide*. Quick.
Quattroruote. *Land Rover: 1948–2008, Sixty Years of Adventure*. Domus.
Rivera, Sheila. *Thunderbird*. ABDO.
Robson, Graham. *Bentley - A Legend Reborn*. Haynes.
Ronicke, Frank. *Trabant 1957–1991*. Motorbuch Verlag.
Ruiz, Marco. *Encyclopedia of the Automobile*. Mondadori.
Seifert, Eberhard. *BMW's Entire History*. Automobilia.
Sessa, O., Clarke, M., Bruni, A., Paolini, F. *The Italian Car*. Giunti.
Wood, Jonathan. *The Rolls Royce*. Shire.
Young, Anthony. *Camaro*. Motorbooks International.
Zumbrunn, M., Cumberford, R. *Cars: Legendary Cars*. Mondadori.
Zumbrunn, M., Heseltine, R. *Ferrari – The Models That Made History*. Mondadori.

Other sources of information:
The Italian magazines *Quattroruote, Ruoteclassiche and Auto Italiana*, published by Domus.
The magazine *AutoCapital*, published by Rizzoli Magazines.
Milleruote – Encyclopedia of the Car, Domus/The De Agostini Geographical Institute.
The public relations sites of Alfa Romeo, Aston Martin, Bentley, BMW, Chevrolet, Chrysler, Citroen, Ferrari, Fiat, Ford, Jaguar, Land Rover, Mercedes, Porsche, Rolls-Royce and Volkswagen.
The websites www.imcdb.org, www.enciclopediadellautomobile.com, www.ultimatecarpage.com.

Acknowledgements

The author thanks Edward Baldi and Marco Coletto. Without their important contribution, this book would not be the same.
The Publisher wishes to thank: Alfa Romeo Press; Aston Martin Media, LLC Chrysler Groups; Fiat Autopress; Franziska Christl and Thomas Peschl, BMW Group Archives; Jens Torner. Porsche AG Press Database, Land Rover, Lorenza Hat and Umberto Gorio, Italdesign Giugiaro SpA Maria Feifel, Daimler Global Media Site, Maurizio Marini, Citroën Communication; Mauro Gentile, Porsche Italy SpA Patrizia Venturini, BMW Group Italy, Rochelle Macdonald, Bentley Motors UK Press; Rolls-Royce Motor Cars Ltd., Trabant, Volkswagen Media.

Index

Photo Credits

METRO BOOKS
New York

An Imprint of Sterling Publishing
387 Park Avenue South
New York, NY 10016

METRO BOOKS and the distinctive Metro Books logo are trademarks of Sterling Publishing Co., Inc.

© 2010 by Edizioni White Star s.r.l.

All rights reserved. No part of this publication may be reproduced, stored in a retrieval system, or transmitted in any form or by any means (including electronic, mechanical, photocopying, recording, or otherwise) without prior written permission from the publisher.

Translation: Salvatore Ciolfi - Editing: John Schaefer
Text: Saverio Villa
Project editor: Valeria Manferto De Fabianis
Editorial coordination:
Laura Accomazzo - Giorgia Raineri
Graphic design: Maria Cucchi

ISBN 978-1-4351-3332-7

For information about custom editions, special sales, and premium and corporate purchases, please contact Sterling Special Sales at 800-805-5489 or specialsales@sterlingpublishing.com.

Manufactured in China

3 5 7 9 10 8 6 4

www.sterlingpublishing.com

288 The air intake on the hood, which has been part of the Cooper S design since 2006, is the main aesthetic distinction of the MINI's sportier version. John Cooper is one of the biggest names in British motorsports, as he also built cars that won the F1 world championship in 1959 and 1960.